D1003091

TWIN POWERS

Politics and the Sacred

by

THOMAS MOLNAR

WILLIAM B. EERDMANS PUBLISHING COMPANY
GRAND RAPIDS, MICHIGAN

With grateful acknowledgment for a grant from
The Earhart Foundation

Copyright © 1988 by Wm. B. Eerdmans Publishing Co.
255 Jefferson Ave. S.E., Grand Rapids, Mich. 49503

Library of Congress Cataloging-in-Publication Data

Molnar, Thomas Steven.
Twin powers: politics and the sacred / by Thomas Molnar.
p.   cm.
ISBN 0-8028-0303-2
1. Religion and politics.   2. Religion and state.
I. Title
BL65.P7M65   1988
320'.01'1—dc19   88-10204
                                            CIP

Contents

*To the memory
of my mother*

Introduction

From the beginning of known time, human communities had, embedded in their self-understanding, a clear conception of their sacred origins. The people believed that their society's origin was sacralized by an act of foundation at a certain place, at a certain time, and by a certain set of rituals; they believed that they and their society were fashioned after some higher model, a divine prototype. Further, they took it for granted that their first ruler was a semidivine figure who had obtained his scepter and his power from the gods. In short, the first ruler over the tribe, the nation, or the empire was thus the connecting link between a higher, permanent reality, understood as more real than this ephemeral and changing world, and the human community here below, a replica of the divine model.

This sacred derivation of power had to be periodically reasserted by means of elaborate rituals which, with their meticulous symbolization, conveyed to both citizens and aliens the privileged standing of the community, its guarantee of enduring, and its protection by greater than earthly powers. Any interruption in the mysterious flow of the originating, meaning-giving, and protecting sacred power would be a grievous event, an irreparable breach in the laws of cosmos and community. Should these foundation-affirming events, gestures, and propitiatory acts in space and time not be subsequently observed by the ruler, by the clergy—indeed, by the entire nation—chaos or nonbeing would reabsorb the community which had been carved out from the surrounding disorder.

Now we must note that, with some variations in different civilizations, what was true of archaic communities has also been true of modern ones. The sacred relationship with a transcendent reality was at all times deeply embedded in the life of every community. The channels with the sacred already mentioned—ruler, clergy, ritual—were supplemented in physical form by such external validations of the community's existence as architecture, music, ceremony, and sacrifices. By creating and sustaining these public symbols, the community could capture and perpetuate the favor of the gods. In this way, the fact of power, political power, manifested itself in the annals of human beings in sacred forms. This was true of the prehistoric ancient world, of the European Middle Ages, and of societies in all corners of the globe—wherever there have been political communities, from the simplest to the most complex. The *sacrality of power* was a universal characteristic of humanity, without exception. While the continuous line of history has displayed a great diversity of political regimes, they have all had one common feature: the sacred character of power, of those who hold power, and of those persons or objects that come in contact with it.

If we wish to grasp the essence of this power as it is exercised and acknowledged, we must understand that the reason why human beings command and obey is to be found ultimately in this sacrality of power that all recognize. There have always been some who try to contradict this truth and suggest alternatives: people obey only under the compulsion of superior force and its naked manifestations; they obey as long as their self-interest dictates it; they obey because rulers occult their judgment by some hypnotizing myth; they obey because they are as yet unenlightened about the ruler's corruption; and the list goes on. The historical records indicate, however, that the strongest cement for community cohesion has always been, as I have stated, the citizens' belief that, one way or another, their community belonged to a reality higher than their own reality as individuals. The power of the state as such—embodied as it is in institutions, laws, statecraft, military strength, and police enforcement—was understood to be a branch of a *superior agency* which stands above the state and uses it as a channel through which to manifest itself.

What I have described here was for long a constant of history; as such it would need little discussion. But the issue grows in importance because sometime in the past few centuries, some thinkers began to question the sacred character of power, then to deny it or cast it aside with indifference. Some observers put the origin of this process of erosion in the fourteenth century—in the nominalism of William of Ockham or in the conciliar theory of Marsilius of Padua. Others speak of the "crisis of European consciousness" around 1715, to use the words of Paul Hazard. Still others locate it in the French Revolution or in the impact of industrialization. But no matter whether we fix the roots of the trend five hundred or two hundred years ago, we are left with the phenomenon of a general desacralization of the state, of political power, of society and its institutions—in fact, of the overall tenor of life. The regimes that have come into existence in more recent history (say in the nineteenth or twentieth centuries) and older regimes that have modernized their structures have abandoned the traditional mold and model almost entirely. Their basic presuppositions exclude the sacred from every aspect of their functioning; their link to a tenuously maintained image of a sacred origin has become a spiritless formality; and their symbolization of fundamental acts of the past has eroded under the impact of a growing preoccupation with present and future.[1]

Yet this does not fully answer the question of whether the regimes of modernity represent a complete break in the immemorial relationship between the community and its foundation in the sacred source. If the community no longer regards itself as a replica of the cosmos and its own reality as the reflection of a more potent one, does it preserve, nevertheless, some receptivity for the sacred by which it might anchor itself in the sea of profane existence? Are our communities, by some recent mutation in the condition of humankind, coming to regard themselves as their own cause, products of their own efforts, self-sufficient in giving them-

1. Note, however, that even the most modern of societies maintain some residual sacred elements. This is manifest at the coronation ceremony of the rulers of England, at the inauguration of American presidents, who swear on the Bible to uphold the Constitution, and at the opening ceremonies of the Olympic Games, when the sacred fire is brought from Olympia.

selves foundation and direction? This *would* mean the elimination of the sacred component from their purview and a total relocation of the criteria of self-assessment—in material success or technological achievement, for example. Such a rejection of the sacred would amount to a vast transformation—indeed a mutation—of politics, both theory and practice.

*   *   *

My task now presents itself with a logical necessity. I will first document what I called the sacred component in the human vision and community and show that our relation to, and call by, the sacred is a central characteristic of our humanity. I believe that we are religious beings, as we are also political and social beings. In the course of discussing this point, we will find that the emanations of the sacred imply the potency of our public political world. This is the sphere in which citizens move, but it is not merely the point of intersection of their individual interests; it is, rather, a sui generis zone, the locus of encounter between human transactions and the vertical impact of transcendent reality.

Next, I will show that power appears in the human world abundantly sacralized in the person of the ruler (tribal chief or emperor), a sacrality which does not turn him into a divine figure but which is instrumental in the all-important process of relating people and territory to the source of the sacred. Thus the ruler's manifestations of sacrality articulate the essential aspects of communal life; he is a hieratic figure whose acts, from coronation to the healing of the sick, channel the potent reality of the sacred to the lower realities of his realm.[2]

It seems now, in the light of scholarship as well as the experience of modernity as it clashes with tradition, that Western civilization has indeed broken with the sacred as a sustaining ground of existence. I shall therefore focus in the last two chapters on the *desacralization of power* and its consequences as they shape the present and reach out into the future. Understandably, I will raise

2. See Marc Bloch, *Les rois thaumaturges* (1924; Paris: Gallimard, 1983), who discusses the power of the kings of France to heal scrofula and other sicknesses.

important questions in these chapters. The central quest is whether power is rooted in the human condition, a thesis combatted by those who envisage with satisfaction its twilight and its apparent readiness to be redistributed among all citizens. Yet, insofar as the nature of community appears to be to represent a power structure and a hierarchy, we must assume that power will continue to be the essential motive in all regimes. The only question is whether power, now without a foundation in the sacred, will remain an ordering principle in society and state or whether it will become a source of disorder and anarchy. We now face at least the appearance of a situation in which power is not founded in a transcendent set of references but is attributed to the will of history or to the ad hoc choice of citizens. In either case, power is explained by the mechanism of its functioning, while the mechanism itself— and the very need for such a self-generated and self-perpetuating power—remains unexplained.

My thesis, then, is that there is a crisis today of the foundation of power, a power separated from its sacred source. This is, in essence, the political problematic of our times.

CHAPTER ONE

The Sacred in Life and Vision

According to important thinkers in diverse fields of contemporary scholarship—in archeology, psychology, the history of religion, the study of myths, symbols, and rites—it is inherent in human nature to have spiritual needs we seek to satisfy outside our narrowly circumscribed selves.[1] There seems to be an economy of the human inner equilibrium which commands an individual and collective orientation toward an external force, an external reality, able to explain the meaning of existence and to guide one in the world here below. Thus many thinkers have concluded that religion is not merely an irrational drive or a superstition (the eighteenth-century assumption) and that it cannot be squeezed within the bounds of reason (Kant's and Lessing's thesis). Rather, they believe that human beings are religious beings as much as, or more decisively than, they are political or economic beings. At any rate, the exclusively mechanistic explanation of how we humans function is a thing of the past.

Despite this new tone toward religion, many people still call religious aspirations a mere varnish on humanity's collectivistic, conformist, and cultural behavior. This in spite of the fact that all societies known to history established themselves in some sort of

1. Not all thinkers agree on the need for this search, however. Some believe that these needs are fulfilled by inner human resources, not by outside forces. God, for these thinkers, is a "projection" of our needs onto an imagined super-reality.

dependence on a higher system of reference, and that we have no justification to regard these societies, no matter how archaic, as less deep and less sophisticated observers of nature, the human psyche, and otherworldly reality than we are. In all these cultures, the vertical relationship to a higher reality completed the horizontal network of existence which, in and of itself, did not seem to respond adequately to all the demands people put to themselves and to the world around them.

The contemporary scholarship I mentioned above took the turn it now follows impelled by dissatisfaction with the positivistic view initiated by Auguste Comte and Herbert Spencer and perfected by the French sociologist Émile Durkheim. For Durkheim and his school, society itself is the kind of impressive totality that can provide its members with basic representations of something higher than the individual. Durkheim's persuasiveness was to a considerable extent due to his adherence to the Kantian thesis that there is, beyond human cognition, a thing-in-itself which dictates moral choices without being reducible to a conceptual analysis. He then went one important step further: the thing-in-itself, which for Kant was an inscrutable source of morality, became for the neo-Kantian Durkheim *society* itself, a phenomenon to be explored by the new science of sociology. Equating the thing-in-itself with society, that is, with a transindividual collective entity, Durkheim brought the religious dimension down to earth, regarding it as powerful enough to compel individual cognition and action. *Society* thus became an ultimate, and its directives turned into moral imperatives.

Along Durkheim's extremely influential line of thought new ideas developed that went beyond as well as against his conclusions. Members of anthropological research teams—a relatively new line of exploration at the time—returned from their travels bringing news of archaic communities in which the beings and objects regarded as sacred were not intracommunitarian, not collective representations, as Durkheim would have it. Society itself did not assume the role of religious source through the collective imagination; rather these societies saw their definition and foundation in some *external* sacred that gave it its being and structure. Various students of the phenomenon called this outside sacred "mana," "the numinous," "the tremendum," or "the holy." While these mysterious entities could not be equated with pagan gods or with the God of monotheistic Middle Eastern religions, they still granted the sacred an independent status. Not only independent, the sacred was also "multiple" because it "covered" life in all its manifestations, even though it was derived from one potent source. The conclusion to be drawn was that in addition to humanity's other dimensions, needs, and aspirations, there is also a religious dimension, manifest regardless of the degree of political organization of a given group.

Add to the sociological and anthropological views a third line of search, represented by depth psychology. Here too, the positivists predominated at the beginning, with Jean-Martin Charcot and Sigmund Freud heading a school which tended to reduce psychic phenomena to anything from chemical reactions to sexual discontent. The point at which psychology joined the search into the sacred came with C. G. Jung, who claimed to have discovered in the individual and collective subconscious whole series of symbols that appeared across civilizational barriers, thus pointing to a common substratum of our deepest needs.

Both Freud and Jung were physicians, and their medical orientation prompted them to elaborate therapies by which patients could be cured by reintegration into a life of normal functioning. Neither could resist the temptation, however, to draw wide-ranging conclusions from his case studies. Freudian therapy, influenced by a positivistic view of what constitutes a good, that is, rational, society, aimed at psychoanalyzing individuals and curing them by bringing them back to rationality and a scientific view of existence. The sum total of the thus cured men and women was to be the social ideal of the future. Jung, on the other hand, focused on what he saw as the individual's dependence on and desired integration with the group, with vast elements and epochs of culture, indeed, with the substratum of humankind's basic symbols. His search thus included the field of religious symbolization, the study of alchemy and hermetism, the quest for archetypal imagery and its subtle influence on one's self-image. Over against Durkheim and Freud, Jung found that humanity's deepest needs were linked to a mysterious presence and its manifold manifestation—both in archaic structure of a tribe, where the mysterious presence plays out its local articulations, and in the life of individuals (not necessarily patients), where it acts as a therapeutic agent.

It fell to Mircea Eliade, among others, to pull the strings of religious scholarship together and, if not actually to discover, at least to delineate the links tying together human beings and their heightened environment permeated by the presence of the sacred. Today, due largely to Eliade's popularization of a century's studies of the sacred, we have before us the story of archaic peoples whose every act in life, and for that matter before and after life, took place in the sacred dimension as much as in the profane. Theirs was no mere nature worship as earlier ethnographers assumed. We must rather speak of a stance in which each of the ever-recurrent events of life was sacralized because it represented—or, better, *was*—part of cosmic permanence and belonged to the structure of reality. Foundations and beginnings were thus regarded as sacred, as were places, times, objects, and rites which marked the intervention of superior powers into the course of profane existence, thereby sacralizing it.

The *style* in which the community's sacred experience expressed itself, including the components of the landscape, the gods, the material substratum, the quest for security and harmony, the existentially real, varied from one community to another; the *experience,* however, was present in each case. In ancient Egypt, Christian Norberg-Schultz observes, buildings represented a synthesis of four fundamental intentions: the enclosed "oasis," the durable, megalithic mass, the orthogonal order, and the path or axis—they were symbolic, in other words, of the Egyptians' cosmic order. Under the later dynasties, architecturally repetitive themes were added, "like the monotonous reiteration of long and formalized prayers for the dead."[2]

In Greece, certain sites where nature seemed to dominate were dedicated to the old chthonic deities Hera and Demeter, and places where the human intellect and discipline complemented and opposed the chthonic forces were dedicated to Apollo. Towns en-

2. Norberg-Schulz, *Meaning in Western Architecture* (New York: Praeger, 1975), 30.

joyed the protection of Athena, while harmony in the forces of life indicated the presence of Zeus. Before a temple was built, open-air altars were erected in the ideal position from which the whole sacred and meaningful landscape could be grasped.

Were there limits separating profane and sacred? Indeed there were, clearly drawn in time, space, and ceremony. Their infringement brought, on the family or community, an immediate retaliation, or at least exclusion from the visible or invisible field of force within which the sacred was seen to be valid and potent. Thus there is a rich literature describing the rites of tribes and cities that inscribed into the fabric of thinking, feeling, and acting the inviolable character of a territory thus designated. In the story of the founding of Rome, for example, Romulus, accompanied by the tribal notables, ploughed all around the future seat of power, lifting the plough only where the future city walls would be interrupted by gates. The rich symbolization of this and related acts gave them a timeless character in several respects. A city-state was to be established in the profane order, but at the same time, according to the law connecting the earthly with the cosmic, a segment of significance was also carved out and separated from the surrounding chaos. This was the sacred order. As this example shows, the sacred and the profane, while separated and delimited, were linked through an act by which the sacred conferred meaning on the profane. Only in this manner can one explain why Romulus struck down Remus when he in defiance jumped over the ploughed furrow, that is, the wall not yet constructed. Remus's leap was interpreted as prefiguring a future enemy assault against the city, and Romulus's murder of his brother—an act of ritual murder—projected a similar fate for all later enemies of Rome.

If we now consider that the foundation act was further surrounded by other symbols, we penetrate more deeply into the nature of the sacred as it guaranteed the integrity and meaningfulness of the profane sphere. Romulus was divinely appointed in preference to Remus as the city's founder. When Jupiter was invoked, he sent twelve eagles (his emblematic animal) to the older brother against only half that number for Remus. Romulus's act of foundation was thus approved by the gods, and the symbol they assigned, the Roman eagle, became that of the army. Nor was even

the shape of the city left to chance. It was a square, like the later
Roman military camps, signifying the most compact configuration; it had a center and equidistantly spaced avenues; and it was
crossed by the *axis mundi,* the axis of the world as imagined by
the ancients or the "cosmic middle." When we look at any number of pre-Christian sacred grounds—at Angkor Vat in Cambodia
or Borobudur in Java, at the pyramids in Egypt or in the Yucatan,
or at the ziggurats in Mesopotamia—we find the same sacred
shape, no matter whether the sacred structure is temple, city, or
royal palace. The reason lies not in architectural facility but in the
fact that the square symbolizes the earth while the circle, as we
shall see later, symbolizes heaven, the perfect, the divine.[3]

C. G. Jung located supreme harmony in the East Asian Tantric
mandala (a circle enclosing a square), and he saw it as the basic
scheme of the design that his patients drew of their own accord on
their way to recovery, that is, as they began to discover their place
in the universe. Whether we find the mandala in a building, a drawing, or even an oriental carpet, the square, the earthly principle,
and the circle, the supramundane one, symbolize by their junction
the completeness of the cosmos, the roots of humanity's integration with the universe, and therefore also the integration and
cooperation of our pulsions and faculties.

It is not easy to scrutinize the interaction between human
beings and external reality, a reality endowed with sufficient
potency to influence them and the course of their existence; but it
is undeniable that the interaction activates the soul, whether in the
form of archaic town building, temple architecture, collective
rites, or cultic or psychic drawings. Eliade points out that the
emanations of the sacred (hierophany) reach humans in various
forms, that they possess specific powers, and that they shape cultures as ordering principles. Consequently, he defines the sacred
as a *kratophany*—emanation of power—manifest in the world in
various forms.

What is the nature of this power, invisible yet able to shape

3. In Western Christendom, only the cross could modify this consecrated shape, as is evident in the grand design of the cathedrals. Even
there, however, the circular way of the cross symbolizes humanity's pilgrim-
age in quest of salvation.

civilizations and endow institutions with a force to which we remain attracted? We shall distinguish two aspects: the sacred as a *reality* and the sacred as a *social dynamic*. The sacred as we experience it is a force transmitted from a source beyond the power itself. While that source—Christianity calls it God—is grasped as reality itself, it is not directly manifest to the senses: we avert our eyes as Moses did on Mount Sinai even while receiving God's revelation.[4] The sacred is then a channel which penetrates our senses, establishing a meaning in what the senses reveal and embedding it in the soul, where it remains even after the transmission through the senses has ceased. Thus the Russians, with a directness that hits the mark, call their icons "windows to God." The sacred, mediating between the supernatural and our openness, is more real than daily facts because it gathers these facts into signifying bundles. It has permanence, stability, power of transmission, and elevating power. It comes closest to what the ancients called *myth,* through which they grasped the structure of being, a being forceful enough to be experienced in tales of universal validity. The sacred, for the ancients and moderns alike, stabilizes the scheme of reality and punctuates the stations of our interpretation of reality. We feel an awe in sacred places and in front of sacred objects, during the performance of sacred rites in sacred time, before gestures consecrated by their transcendent significance. This is not an empty emotionalism, an appeal to credulity. It has, as its correspondent, a reality more real than what we generally call reality. The unembraceable divinity is present through the sacred; it is through the sacred that it transmits a force it does not employ in contact with humble forms of life. To use the words of Eliade, the sacred *stops* before sacralizing the profane, before it encroaches on the latter's territory.

The other face of the sacred is turned toward humanity. The sacred manifestation is not an individual affair; it is essentially communal. True, God reveals himself to great mystics and prophets, to Moses, Paul, and Francis, but this was done directly, without

4. Walter Otto has written intriguing pages on how the Greeks found in their gods and goddesses embodiments of the way reality worked in their lives; see, for example, *Dionysius, Myth, and Cult,* trans. Robert B. Palmer (Bloomington: Indiana University Press, 1965).

the mediation of a sacred channel. Further, it was always understood that those to whom God revealed himself would then bring
the good news and its tangible effects to a collectivity, to the rest
of humanity. Even private places of worship, the corner in Roman
homes for the Penates and Lares (Christianity was to call them
"guardian angels"), were not literally private: they served a house-
hold within a system of beliefs, not an individual alone. Likewise
it would be foolish to imagine Christian hermits and anchorites organizing rites of their own invention and use. The sacred addresses
itself to a potentially universal assembly, universal at least within
the confines of a given pantheon.

We have seen that a community does not regard itself as truly
constituted until a sacred beginning is ascribed to it. Children become aware of their individuality and personhood only long after
birth, when, at the age of three or four, they perceive themselves
as distinct unities. A collectivity, on the other hand, a tribe or a nation, must know its identity at once.[5] The example of Rome's
founding is only one of many. It seems that the *fact* of community requires a very precise coordination of sacred and profane; the
two cooperate in order to give the emerging communal entity a
graspable consciousness, a means of orientation in time and space
here in the concrete but also simultaneously in the dimension of
ontological reality, in the cosmos. Every major act of the community will thereafter embrace the totality of the past with the help
of commemorative events, ceremonies, symbols, and gestures, in
a rich register for the senses, including national anthems, flags,
poems, legends and myths, burial places, and battlefields. An invisible society of a moral-social character is placed above the tangible society, as it were, inseparable from it, explaining it to new
generations, and blocking it to aliens.

In the so-called archaic times, the reaffirmation of communi-

5. The question of identity is answered in the life of every community.
At a primitive level, the identifying tag is simply *man,* as if the humanity of
members of a given group distinguished them from other groups. The term
Inuit, the true name of the Eskimo, means "man," and the same is true of
the term *Bantu* in Africa. American blacks also address each other as "man."
The label is also a founding term: "men" are the first humans, God's first
creations.

ty founding and communal reality used to be done by periodic rites which reenacted the foundation events of gods and heroes, thus reasserting the social identity and cleansing it of the annual accumulation of sins (that is, the breaking of the ties with the cosmos) committed by individual members or by the collectivity as a whole. This was not an exclusively political or even religious performance. The periodic and meticulously organized ensemble of dances, gestures, and sacrifices reanimated the community in contact with the cosmic model; it reconnected the microcosm here below to the macrocosm of universal dimensions. The humanly circumscribed reality of the tribe was once more and repeatedly bathed in the gods' vivifying presence, in their exemplary reality.[6]

We have found that the sacred belongs to a sphere of mediation between the ultimate real (or the creator of the real) and the human world. Hence it is the greatest reality to which we have access with human means. Our rational faculties alone are clearly not adequate to know and fathom it. Our analytical tools, when applied to the sacred, dissolve their object in the process of scrutiny. By the "reality of the sacred" we therefore mean a domain that demands unique approaches not available to the individual. On closer reflection, we will see that this is not as surprising as it first appears.

*   *   *

In anticipation of later chapters, we can also note here that there is another area incommensurable with the individual: politics. Except in careless speech, it is meaningless to say "individual politics," for one cannot speak of individuals, either in their capacity as participants in the political process or in their capacity as leaders, in separation from the community. On the other hand, we

---

6. René Girard, a contemporary student of the sacred, suggests that the founding act had to be a murder which subsequently would be ritualized and performed again and again in bloody ceremonies so as to keep away any further internal violence from the tribe. The victim thus became a scapegoat, carrying the burden of the community's "original sin" and reminding its members of the licit and illicit. The victims were originally chosen from members of the community; later on, according to Girard, they were replaced by slaves or prisoners of war; later yet by animals.

can speak of a good or moral man, though scarcely of a moral community.[7]

Politics refers to a communal activity—it makes sense only as such. So it is with the sacred. Our first and fundamental perception of it is that it becomes manifest as a vast, overwhelming reality and presence. It is unexplainable, as are the manifestations of power in the political sphere. Reflecting upon the latter, we ask: Who or what has instituted it over us? Why do we obey its injunctions? What are its limits? What is the secret of its everpresence among human beings? With the sacred, matters are, strangely, simpler, because we do not ask the first question: Who brought it to us? We know the answer: a superior power whose impact is simultaneous with its presence, although this presence is in some ways "inside" the sacred object or ceremony. Pope Gregory VII expressed it very simply when he warned simoniacs against selling objects of the cult: The sacred objects, he wrote in 1081, serve the sanctuaries and the altars. They are sacred because they have the Holy Spirit in them.

Things become clear as we analyze the communal acts of translating the invisible sacred into tangible or perceivable forms such as buildings, music, sanctuaries, sacred cities, urban design, myth-making, or temple or church construction. We may see illustrations in such widely differing sites as the ziggurats of Mesopotamia, the temple of Karnak in Egypt, Borobudur in Java, the Aztec pyramids, the cities or ruins of Delphi, Mecca, Benares, Jerusalem, Rome, and many others. Such sites possess, of course, a rich, partly mythical, past but also a historical past, the two having fused long ago. What is important in plumbing the meaning of such sites, however, is not so much the archeological or chronological discoveries of analytical scholarship but the beliefs

---

7. "The free choice of individuals, who think they decide what is best for them," wrote Hegel, "is but an illusory independence." *Principles of the Philosophy of Law,* 181. Today the statement has totalitarian implications, yet Hegel did not say more than Adam Smith, whose writings he knew. Both have in mind the interdependence of members of the civil society who, as transactions of all sorts become increasingly complex and intersecting, lose awareness of where individual decision ends and social good (or harm) begins.

and behavior of masses of people in a time which has lost its temporality through the interaction of the community and the sacred. The continuing interaction is then *simultaneous* with the original act as well as with the interactions of successive generations of believers in the past and future. It is a link with the permanent, a timeless significance carved out from the surrounding darkness and chaos.

All sacred acts emphasize and gain meaning from the simultaneity of the original act and subsequent reenactments, timeless immersions in a supernatural reality. The child is baptized or initiated in an act that becomes one with the original act as well as with the long line that has issued from it. The Moslem kisses the Kaaba stone which reaffirms his membership in Allah's grace and the Islamic community. In Benares, hundreds of corpses wrapped in white linen are conveyed each day to the shores of the Ganges, there to be burned and the ashes thrown into the waters of the sacred river. In Rome or at the cathedral of Chartres, the remains of former sacred edifices serve as foundations of the present buildings. Although they belong to a variety of sacred spheres, including pre-Christian ones, they reinforce each other. What is true of the immemorial succession of buildings and sites, through which the sacred presence creates simultaneity of the *then* and the *now,* is true also of liturgies, forms, gestures, music, and ritual dance. They may be called mobile forms of the sacred, yet they too are permanent reenactments of the original movements and words.

This atemporal fusion that the sacred embodies suggests the invisible presence of a model that must be copied, imitated, reproduced, and adhered to. The greater the conformity to it here below—that is, the greater the reenactment of or immersion in it— the more the community is assured of its borrowed permanence, its permeation by the reality of the original. We saw how Romulus founded Rome, how he shaped the *urbs*[8] on the sacred model, implicitly endowing it with power and duration as the work of the gods. At the other end of the earth we find similar concepts in the

---

8. *Urbs* is related to *orbis,* a sphere, and the spherical shape always denoted a rounded totality—the "primordial egg," the womb, etc. The city is thus a self-contained whole, the origin of all things.

building of the Angkor Vat temple complex. Bernard Groslier, a former curator of the temple, speaks of the Khmer's integrated view of the universe. In Angkor, he writes, this was reflected by a harmonious combination of a powerful political organization, a strong, centralized, and uniform society, and a fabulous technical organization for rice cultivation. Spread over these elements was an artistic genius and deep religious belief. If we look at aerial photographs of Angkor and at charts based on them, we see put into practice the same principle used at Rome—what may be described as the mandala principle. According to Giuseppe Tucci, "a mandala is a consecrated area kept pure for ritual and liturgical ends, but it is also a map of the cosmos. . . . It is a geometric projection of the world reduced to an essential pattern. . . . It is a psychocosmogram, the scheme of disintegration from the One to the Many and of reintegration from the Many to the One."[9] This explains why Jung attributes such an importance to the observation that his patients draw mandalas on the way to recovery from mental and spiritual dispersion.

We find the same preoccupation in sacred areas and buildings, which embody a pattern which is not haphazardly traced but which serves primarily as a replica of cosmic design. Since the cosmos is the highest reality observable by the senses, the participants in a given sacred sphere know they are integrated with the highest reality: through this integration, they obtain their own reality, heightened as they see around themselves the same pattern reproduced. The psychic, the tangible, and the cosmic equilibrium thus respond to each other.

Take as an illustration of the fusion of these elements the recent consecration of a Catholic church near Clermont, France. The four-hour ceremony, accompanied by Gregorian chant, was finally culminated by a mass celebrated by the bishop. After the ancient formula of supplication addressed to the saints, the bishop placed relics inside the altar. The master builder then cemented the opening. In place are now relics of St. Louis, St. Francis of Sales, and St. Amator, a Roman martyr of the first century. The bishop then

9. Tucci, *The Theory and Practice of the Mandala* (London: Rider, 1961), 23.

sang the consecration prayer: "May this place be forever sacred and this table ready to receive Christ's sacrifice. . . ." The rites which followed struck the imagination, likening the church building to a living person. Just as the baptized infant receives unction with the consecrated oil, the church, together with the altar, was anointed at twelve places on the wall where crosses will hang with candles burning before them.

The bishop poured the sacred oil on the four corners of the altar and spread it out on the surface with his bare hand. He then toured the church and stopped under every cross and repeated: "May this temple be sanctified in the name of the Father, the Son, and the Holy Spirit." When he returned to the altar, he placed incense on it and lit it, so that the entire surface was on fire, consuming the consecrated oil. Then followed the consecration of the rest of the building.

Another example is the Buddhist temple Borobudur in Java. In connection with the recent work of restoration of this immense, 1200-year-old edifice, schematic maps and diagrams have been drawn of the sanctuary. One is struck by the mandala design, the concentration of all the elements of the temple as the explication and exploration of one seminal idea: concordance with a divine reproduction as the itinerary for the worshiper. The temple consists of eight concentric squares which point to three concentric circles at their center. At the center of these is the great stupa, a stylized "sacred mountain" whose summit communicates with the gods. (Similar mounds are found in the old Burmese city of Pagan, where hundreds of them form sacred ruins extending over many square miles as an enormous sanctuary.)

This is one symbolic dimension of the Borobudur temple. The other, the concentric quadrangles and circular terraces, symbolizes the labyrinthine ways through which one must pass before reaching rebirth—nirvana, the liberation from all worldly attachments. The itinerary of liberation is also traced in the stone walls themselves: each square represents a part of the cycle of birth and rebirth, the cause of the misery of the human condition. The teaching is evident, and the pilgrim, passing from one stage to another, leaves behind both a symbolic and a material obstacle on the way to union with the ineffable.

As with Angkor Vat and Borobudur, so with medieval Cistercian art. As Georges Duby writes,

> The cloister is situated at the orthogonal intersection of the axes of the universe. Stretched on the cross of the four cardinal points, the cloister becomes like an immense cadran [the face of a clock] where all the rhythms of the cosmos allow themselves to be captured. . . . The cloister reduces the world's agitation and confusion to the regularity of the spirit, to the slow progression toward the Eternal, approached by the convert to Christian life in love and humility. . . . The square courtyard is the crossroads of the universe. In its center there stands man, alone capable of grasping the process, the laws and the goal of creation, since he is made on God's image.[10]

These are but a few illustrations of what constitutes the world of the sacred. At every point we find the consciousness of a reality placed between God and humanity, not as a screen or an obstruction but as a mediator. Without the sacred, we may still know God, but he would have to illumine the soul at every stage, he would have to be born and reborn in it for every act of worship. But human beings are not made that way. When God enjoins the people in Deuteronomy to love him with all their heart, with all their soul, and with all their might, he also signifies that all human faculties and senses must be enlisted in the act of worship. Here enters the function of the sacred which is not a disembodied spirit floating above humanity but a many-dimensioned assemblage, bearing a significance and an evocative power related to all human acts. Whether one seeks annihilation of the self at Buddhist temples or beatitude at Cistercian monasteries, individual salvation events, nourished and facilitated by the sacred, are woven into a collective act. The temple and the monastery are themselves products and expressions of the collective turning to the ultimate reality—not as ends but as ways and channels.

For this reason the sacred is not a single manifestation; rather, it comes to our awareness as a network of symbols. One who listens to Bach's music is able to call forth sacred symbols of a dif-

---

10. Duby, *Saint Bernard et l'art cistercien* (Paris: Flammarion, 1979), 130-31.

ferent nature, symbols that penetrate through other senses. In such moments, a unity and a harmony are established, assured by a common source to which all symbols refer. These networks of symbolization are not arbitrary affairs; one does not move the same part of the soul as the other does. Wagner's music does not bring forth the experience of the unity of divine presence. It evokes, rather, the formidable power and turbulence of nature, or, when it is soothing, the play of animals and fairies on a sun-lit forest clearing. To the Christian ear it is an enthusiastically pagan music, touching very different registers of the soul than does Bach or Gregorian chant. The latter is the musical rendering of the slow itinerary of the soul that we find in space and in stone in the ambulatories of monasteries.

Architecture and music, twin arts in both the sacred and the profane registers, are privileged revealers of the sacred. They provide symbols of our deepest roots in space and time, which explains why every civilization—every area of symbolization, one might say—is a new ordering of these two intimate realities. In this sense, architecture and music contain both glories and dangers, because their manipulation or modification brings vast changes in the world-picture they symbolize and promote—as Plato well understood when he excluded certain rhythms from his ideal republic. We said of architecture and its extension urban design that they mirror deep requirements of the soul. In traditional cultures, the temple and the city are situated at the intersection of sacred and profane; they are paradigmatic places located in the *axis mundi* and reproducing the celestial archetype. Music has a similarly public and paradigmatic function, as if time and space could be harmonized through it. Like architecture, music is meant to initiate dialogue with the suprahuman reality, with the cosmic or divine. Its rhythm can express and impose either a circular or a linear movement on humanity's inner being, passions, and desire for cosmic immobility. Just as ancient cities and temples or medieval churches reflect the *imago mundi,* so too music, archaic and medieval, is circular, that is, repetitive, endless, returning to itself. The music in tribal African or American Indian communities does not seek the endless sexual arousal of the discotheques of the Western world. Rather, when it stimulates the participants to a frenzy, then to exhaustion, its goal is a loss of individuality and absorption into the world above, a more real world.

One could make similar observations about sacred objects in general. A Gothic church may thus be interpreted as a sacred language. The cruciform edifice is so constructed as to symbolize the Christ-man, the mediator par excellence. Students of art and religion, including Geoffrey Scott, Bernard Berenson, Mircea Eliade, and Hans Sedlmayr, have called attention to the necessary humanity and human analogy of sacred art. We speak of art in terms of bodily inclinations and motions when we say, for example, that "spires soar," "domes swell" or "arches spring"; that a colonnade "invites" us to walk down its length; or that a classical building "leads us" to its center. Michelangelo made a wise observation when he said that to master the human figure is to comprehend architecture.

This human-relatedness (and this includes the sacred orientation) is present also in Islamic art, although Islam's view of humanity is quite different from the Christian view. According to Titus Burckhardt's ingenious observation, the floor plan of a mosque is very different from that of a Christian church. It is nonarticulated and amorphous, symbolizing human existence which, in itself, is a random course, comprehensible only by reference to the will of Allah. The Gothic church, in contrast, has at its center a nave which, as Eliade remarks, expresses the spiritual and physical sensation of being transported in a closed receptacle in an unlimited element—ocean or eternity. The word *nave,* in fact, comes from the Greek *naos,* "ship." The nave, the transept, and the other principal areas of the building form Christ's body on the cross, with his head resting on the altar. Gothic architecture, and Western church architecture in general, thus says: *ecce homo:* Christ the incarnate and all men.[11] The ambulatory too is full of meaning: it represents the way of the pilgrim or *viator,* the traveler from cradle to grave, from the world to eternity, but also from home to the sacred shrine.

Islamic sacred language is different: it does not refer to an incarnate God at its spiritual center. Perhaps for this reason it is less

11. The basilica, of Eastern origin, symbolizes the cosmos in its Greco-Christian circularity. Hence the insistence in the Eastern church on Christ's enlarged presence as the Pantocrator.

intellectual, as the amorphous plan of the mosque also suggests. Burckhardt sees in the arabesque "a surface transformed into a tissue of colors, a vibration of light and shadow" behind which there is a religious intention. The endless intertwining of the lines "hinders the mind from fixing itself on any particular form, from saying 'I' as an image says 'I.' The center of an arabesque is everywhere and nowhere; each affirmation is followed by a negation."[12] In other words, while Christianity tolerates a great amount of anthropomorphism and calls attention to the self as the center of creation and as itself a creator as well as the locus of meditation, Islam humbles the self, melts it down, so to speak, in the rhythm and pulsation of the world as ordained by Allah. There are here two languages of the sacred. While they both embrace the human and the divine, their expressions reveal vastly different premises and contrasting grammars.

Hinduism provides yet a third language and grammar. The main impression one gets before Hindu monuments is that of proliferating forms—rich vegetation, teeming animal and human life—in stone, painting, carpets, and jewelry. I do not mean, of course, the Taj Mahal with its pure lines and surfaces; that is Islamic art of the seventeenth century. I mean rather the temples and shrines of Benares, Bhubaneswar, and other Hindu sacred places. Such a proliferation of statuary would be an affirmation of life in the European baroque; in Hinduism, however, it is the negation of life, a statement of the unreality of being, of indifference to the one or the many.

We may draw a most important conclusion from these illustrations. The sacred used to be present in all cultures, despite the culture's presuppositions. The thrust of Egyptian and Greek temple art was to come to terms with the cosmos, nature, and the ideal site, so as to give humanity existential security. Christian churches, on the other hand—Western, Byzantine, and Russian—were indifferent to the surrounding world from which no salvation, no existential security could be obtained. Hence the often cursory treat-

12. Burckhardt, "Perennial Values in Islamic Art," in *The Sword of Gnosis: Metaphysics, Cosmology, Tradition, Symbolism,* ed. Jacob Needleman (Baltimore: Penguin, 1974), 312. Visitors of the Alhambra in Granada can testify to the pertinence and sensitive grasp of these observations.

ment of the exterior, at least in the early centuries. All efforts were reserved for entering worshipers, who, on entering, found themselves in a different world, one of significance and splendor. Grace from God was not the same as harmony with the world outside.

We find, then, that in all traditional art, time and space are not haphazardly or pragmatically conceived and randomly executed but that their meaningful articulation serves as a background for the functions of the sacred and its symbols. Eliade and René Guénon emphasize the ubiquity of symbols in the religions and civilizations they have investigated. In the pre-Christian cosmos of all cultures, almost everything could be a sign and could refer in turn to any other sign. In such a cosmos, in which all the parts were interdependent, people survived spiritually, and also physically, by magic—that is, by manipulating parts of the inferior world through talismans and amulets in order to achieve the desired goal in the superior world, among the celestial bodies. Thus symbols and signs, objects, ritual gestures, magical manipulations, and finally humans themselves constituted in the pre-Christian universe a unified yet diversified field, a compact, self-engendered, continuous, and self-explanatory sacred. The advantage of this archaic view, which Guénon identifies with the Great Tradition of immemorial origin, is the unfailing orientation it offers to us, together with the meaning it provides objects and events around us. In such a universe there is no surprise; the seemingly new blends with the old, the habitual, the already experienced. It is well described as the world of "eternal return" and "cyclic time," a world-picture of basic immobility in which individual, tribe, and empire fulfill a transcendent assignment and cannot be assaulted by the shocks (Eliade calls it "terror") of temporality, of the unforeseen, of history. As Paul Wheatley observes, the ancient city, the political entity, functioned as an *axis mundi* about which the state revolved, itself laid out as an *imago mundi* in order to ensure the protection and prosperity of the living, the dead, and the not-yet born.[13]

*   *   *

13. Wheatley, *City as Symbol* (London: H. K. Lewis, 1969), 20.

Now it may seem to some modern readers that throughout these pages I have illustrated only an archaic worldview. They find themselves unfamiliar with the forest of symbols described; they perhaps see only an immense rupture between two conceptions, the archaic and the modern. The towns in which they live are functionally built, without regard to the shape and height of buildings, among which it is almost impossible to distinguish the church, the school, the hospital, the law court, and the factory. These buildings thus evidently symbolize nothing. The town builders ignored everything about the *imago mundi;* the urbanist's blueprint did not lay out the main square as the intersection of axes from the cardinal points. As the inharmonious layout, so the music played in studios and concert halls: the loud and the sultry tones, the drawn-out cries and screeching noises, the wild anarchic rhythm—all is produced to bring immediate tension, relief, then tension again to the animal instincts, just as contemporary canvasses in museums and galleries stress the shapeless, the roaring color patch, or the cool, unemotional machine and bare geometric lines.

Modern humanity's other activities are similarly disconnected from the structured pattern and the meaningful model. In the environment created by the urbanist's and engineer's brutal lines and by the composer's discordant notes, commercial, educational, and political activity appears self-seeking, locked in an ad hoc, mechanistic pseudo-satisfaction in strange contrast to the breathless tempo with which we pursue our fragile aims. An even greater contrast exists between our compressed state in megalopolises, classes, commercial centers, and public transport and the solitude we each feel as a lone unit of a mass, reduced to a standardized existence, calling forth frightful bureaucratic apparatuses as depersonalized organizational principles.[14]

In view of this, we may measure our turnabout when we compare the belief in previous times of the divinely willed foundation

14. It may be useful to recall the Kafkaesque literature which brings all these elements home to us, for which the moderns have invented a telling term, *Angst* or *anguish,* which is neither fear of an identifiable source of danger nor disquiet, which may be an objectless mood. Anguish is a state of dislodgment from the satisfying set of archetypes, from the "home" offered by integration with archaic symbols.

of the community with the modern concept that societies are instituted by contract, based on nothing but individual interest.
Tradition used to have it that the meticulous reenactment of the
message implicit in the cosmic pattern and in the mundane replica
would secure the rules of behavior in the community. In the con-
tracted modern society, it is the interplay and reciprocal friction of
interests which are automatically supposed to engender behavior.
The main characteristic of this situation is its total separation from
the sacred, as if suddenly (writers date it in various epochs or
events) a link had broken, or corrosion had set in inside the cos-
mos-centered world picture. Louis Dumont speaks of the "cosmic
legitimation of the world," the consequence of the denial that there
may be anything "ontologically real outside the individual."[15] Eric
Voegelin sees the first signs of the derailment in the twelfth-cen-
tury southern Italian abbot Joachim of Flore and his division of
history into "three ages." René Guénon finds the beginning of decline in William of Ockham's nominalism, in the "quantification"
of a worldview based on a qualitatively articulated heaven. Henry
Corbin indicts, as the fundamental turnaway from the divine to the
human, the Christian Incarnation. Nietzsche and Heidegger go
back even further, to Socrates and Plato and the equation of
humanity with the exclusively rational, the "oblivion of Being."

Without pursuing this and parallel lines of speculation (the
third chapter is devoted to them on another plane), let us focus on
the sacred and its significance. I have already noted the communitarian character of the sacred. Yet, in contrast to the modern collective concept which seeks sociological bases and the concilia-
tion of self-interest with efficiency, the traditional concept of the
sacred always refers to a reality beyond itself. Within the sacralized universe, the lower reality—no matter how lofty its temple
cities, no matter how tuned to the soul its rhythm—remains a
humble replica of the higher. The sacred itself is an expression of
this distance. More, it settles inside this distance, this space,
whereby it may exert its function. Above lie the ultimate mysteries; below, the efforts to capture them in a lasting way in the form
of safe roots, stability, and equilibrium. The world below obtains

15. Dumont, *Essais sur l'individualisme* (Paris: Seuil, 1983), 58, 73.

these blessings through openness to emanations from the world above, through conformity (always threatened by human imperfection) to the nature of absolute reality. For the community to be harmonious and prosperous, it must articulate itself—its cities and temples, but also its public life—according to the celestial model in which vast, powerful, even contrary forces move in interaction.[16] This capturing of the cosmic or divine secret is the ultimate task of emperors, kings, founders, tribal chiefs, and officials. They are themselves sacred insofar as they have not only grasped the secret but also become spiritually and physically integrated with the higher sphere as living channels between the perfect reality above and the imperfect reality of earthly arrangements.

A good illustration is the sacred significance assumed by the Mundang king in Africa. He is in charge of his kingdom's relations both with the surrounding world and with past events. He must maintain unity and preserve society from all excess. All the while, he obeys strict obligations and interdicts; his demarche is stately, his movements slow, his posture quasi-immobile, his face impassible like a mask. All this imitates the majesty of the cosmos and the forces of the earth which are localized in him and provide him with means of action. His actions direct the community's fertility: he makes the rains fall and directs the cycle of growth. His palace is understood as a microcosm. Thus the king is a kind of superhuman monster yet at the same time a mediator-guardian, a beneficent power, the incarnation of the community.

It is understandable that (modern) communities that claim to have been founded by rational human beings and rational criteria and that pursue their course on the assumption that human beings and their transactional relationships are the only reality radically deny the relevance, indeed, the reality, of another order, another

16. Eugenio Garin speaks of city planning in the Renaissance, when architects like Leonardo Bruni and some townspeople, the Florentines, for example, wanted to establish "the small, just city in which all inequalities were remedied by the provisions of rational laws." Bruni's ideal town, Garin writes, was substantially identical with the one drawn by Plato in the sixth book of the *Laws,* with concentric circles (the celestial orbits) around the agora and public buildings. Garin, *Science and Civic Life in the Italian Renaissance* (New York: Doubleday, Anchor, 1969), 30.

model, as well as its accessibility through sacred instruments. For moderns, this cosmic original or system of reference has entirely ceased to be. The human situation is perceived, in consequence, as detached from any hypothetical universal order—not because our contemporaries distrust any such order (in fact, our science regards the universal laws as unassailable) but because this universal order, traditionally understood, rested on a living and thus nonrationalistic and nonmechanical cosmos. Any influence, emanation, or replicating power is denied the old cosmos. It is devalued as anthropomorphic, belonging to the realm of superstition. The consequence of this conceptual shift and the cosmological shift behind it has been that the community, now understood as the mere multiplication and juxtaposition of individuals, came to be regarded as its own cause, and individuals were seen as the sole reality and the sole judge of their and the community's "values." Society is henceforth understood as the product of individual wills. In order to avoid clashes, these wills enter upon a contractual arrangement—revocable in principle but binding while it lasts—of basically gratuitous laws set up according to temporary interests.[17]

Such an autonomous society seeks emancipation from the cosmos or the divine, hence it does not acknowledge its need of the sacred. Yet, as we shall see in Chapter Three, it nevertheless models itself, perhaps unwittingly, on a cosmology, on the modern view of heaven as a homogeneous empty space. The great question is, then, the following: Has Christianity itself fallen victim to the present desacralization; did it perhaps even sponsor the new cosmology? In other words, does Christianity contain a credible and effective sacred?

The sacred is a universal, divine-human reality, and every religion makes room for it in all its manifestations. Christianity is no exception: its liturgy, art, churches, legends, saints, literature, and public festivities all provide occasions to affirm the mysteries of creation, the presence of Christ, and the role of the sacraments in the life of faith and salvation. Every one of these rites, places, times, and formulas is enriched by the sacred's inspiration of ar-

17. The modern advocate of this view is Hans Kelsen, the German legal scholar. I shall speak more of him in Chapter Six.

tistic expression, which blends with the dogmatic and doctrinal corpus it is called upon to represent, signify, and symbolize. The one decisive distinction from other religions and symbolizations resides in the dogma of the Incarnation. Indeed, while the archaic tradition proposed a living cosmos with a multitude of gods, spirits, and daemons at all levels of being, entering the lives of human beings at every juncture and channeling the sacred in a great variety of forms and myths, Christianity sees the universal vitality not spread through the cosmos but concentrated in the incarnate God-Man. The Christ is the *axis mundi;* the story of his birth is the one reference point of all other and later Christian stories, whether legends or documented events; and the cross replaces the intersection of cosmic forces. More than that, through the Incarnation Christ is now the only mediator between the divine and the human (others receive their power only through him). He is the truly sacred channel, present and mediating in every sacrament, in the Mass and its central elevation, the Eucharist. He is also present in artistic expressions, from roadside crucifixes to the pattern of cathedrals, from the retelling and reenacting of the birth at Bethlehem to Dante's grandiose composition.

Christianity also presents another side, however, and this has been amply noted by its critics from the beginning. Over against the archaic tradition with its extremely rich cosmos, Christianity sees all the sacred of the universe concentrated and absorbed in God, leaving nothing to nature, to the celestial sphere, to the underworld, or to the wanderings of the individual soul. The sacred always refers to the one master: nature is denuded of significance, the stars of their mystery, the soul of its explorations outside the severe dialectic of sin and redemption. Dante catches the souls in hell, bitterly complaining about their fate under the divine judge whose will is substituted for the fallible weakness of all. In short, the critics assert that the net effect of Christianity was to desacralize the world, to abolish its drama and myth, and to replace the semi-divine celestial bodies with inert stones. Whatever used to live and exert an influence over human destiny was judged to be an idol. The revered or dreaded forces of the ancient tradition were exposed as pagan superstition and magic. Even more devastatingly, Christianity extended the logic of the Incarnation—God becoming a human being—and suggested that the process might be reversed and humanity might become God. This authorized a strange new being—divinized humanity—to claim absolute domination over history, nature, and the soul. The argument against the Christian religion, in sum, is that it profaned the world, it stripped the cosmos and nature of the mythicopoetic presence with which traditional religion saw it filled. Through the Incarnation, Christianity elevated humanity, all people together with their mundane concerns, to the level of the divine.

Those who thus charge Christianity point to cascading consequences. For a long time, Semitic and pagan—Celtic, Indo-Germanic, Latin, and Hellenic—forms of sacredness survived in the incompletely Christianized cultures of Europe and the Mediterranean.[18] Now, however, with the general enfeeblement of Christianity (which is variously ascribed to the Vatican Council, various splits, mushrooming theologies, and the invasion of oriental sects), the pagan forms reassert themselves.[19] In any case, Christianity had already prepared its own desacralization by extending the implications of incarnation to the processes of historical interpretation, to institutions, and finally to social mores and individual choice. As Henry Corbin argues, the reality of incarnation authorized church and state to humanize history, to dissolve the sacred in the profane, and then to leave all fields of endeavor to the latter. In the present era, which many view as "post-Christian," humanity suffers from the loss of the Christian sacred; the result is that trivial endeavors now become fraudulently sacralized: consumer goods, sex, entertainment, sport, ideological programs, and even media events. Harvey Cox diagnosed it well, labeling as "sacred" whatever strikes people's fancy for more than a day.

To conclude, let us note that Christianity seems to bear an ambiguous attitude vis-à-vis the sacred. In its dogmatic entrails, it had prepared the instruments of desacralization, since the creator God

18. For details, see Sigrid Hunke, *Europas eigene Religion. Der Glaube der Ketzer* (Europe's own religion: The belief of the heretics) (Bergisch-Gladback: Gustav Lubber, 1980).

19. For an extensive discussion see my book, *The Pagan Temptation* (Grand Rapids: Eerdmans, 1987).

tolerates no rival gods, daemons, or independent forces. This God also affirms an absolute guardianship over the soul and mastery over material nature. No spirits push the astral bodies in their orbits; no voice addresses us from the sea or from trees and rocks. The universe is silent, unless it sings its creator's praises through its beauty and harmony.

Yet the Christian desacralization did not become "operational" for more than a millennium after Christ. Christian thinkers, at least up to the time of the Scholastics, populated the universe with hierarchies, allegories, and active forces, all, of course, subordinate to God's judgment, will, and charity. Dante's poem, this grand synthesis of medieval thought, vision, and sensitivity, was the last monument, together with the Gothic cathedral, to give full voice to the Christian worldview still permeated by the sacred.

Then, shortly after Dante's time, the desacralizing side of Christianity emerged. Let us not now debate whether it was late Scholasticism, William of Ockham, or the rise of the burgher class which provided the impetus. In any case, a new physics and a new cosmology, already contained in the Hebrew and Christian vision of creation, asserted themselves in the processes of a contingent universe and in the strong monotheism facing the idols.

Since the fourteenth century, then, the pagan tradition has lain defeated (although not eliminated), but the price was high: a secularized Christian civilization. The vision of the sacred has not been liquidated, yet the secular view has had time to gain a foothold in modern culture, and it now coincides with the public square of modernity. The Christian sacred is in eclipse; it has ceased to operate in the life of Western nations.

CHAPTER TWO

Sacralized Power

Karl Kerényi, the great student of Greek religion and culture, insists in several of his essays that a distinction be made between the Christian *faith* and the *sense of reality*[1] that rises spontaneously toward the transcendent in ancient religion. One has faith in something that is not yet or is departed but expected to return; thus one has faith in a promise, in a presence which is as yet absent, including the divinity of Christ, his resurrection, and the coming eschaton. Such faith is not of the order of a rational certitude, but it is also more dynamic than a mere grasp of fact or evidence since it mobilizes the energies of the soul, keeping them in an alert state. Faith goes together with important emotions and enthusiasms. It also has a permanent desire to find support in the concrete, yet it is not at root disappointed with the concrete's elusiveness.

The "feeling (or sense) of reality," on the other hand, which Raffaele Pettazzoni called the "power of substance" (*"forza sostanza"*), implies the availability of an evidence which strikes us with its own nonderived force, without any major effort on our part. For the ancients, then, the sacred was not so much something to be believed in; it was simply *there* as a matter of unquestioned reality. Unquestioned because it was supported by two undeniable sources: our experience of surrounding nature and the daily observation of our own and other people's psychic motives.

1. For "sense of reality" Kerényi uses the German word *Erlebnis,* which may be also rendered as "intimate experience," but for which there is no adequate term in English.

This is why ancient religion, inseparable from ancient culture as a vision of nature and human destiny, created a sacred realm represented by a pantheon of gods closely present to humanity. This sacred realm was as continuous and seamless as nature itself, though it too, like nature, was sometimes rent by clashes and conflicts—thus clashes in the lives of the gods. These gods, more or less clearly outlined, were not focuses of contradiction but archetypes, recognizable and easily transposable into mythology and statuary. The ancients' theogony, the account of the origin of the gods, concided with their cosmogony, their account of the origin of the entire cosmos. Whatever preceded this double origin was not of great import to ancient religion since it was usually regarded as only darkness and chaos leading up to the real story: the *gesta deorum* in which humanity too subsequently participated. Almost all Greek literary works thus illustrate three stages of myth and reality: theogony, theomachia (the war of the gods), and human participation. The story of Prometheus is an excellent example, pulling together the three motives.

At no point does faith have a function in ancient religion. The sense of the reality and presence of the sacred was strong enough to support what may not even be called a religion in our sense of the term. This does not exclude the concept of transcendence, however. On the contrary, if the transcendent is the objective reality, the horizon of human vision, then the sense of reality must be understood as confidence in powers beyond the subjective soul, powers which invest the soul with larger-than-human contents. In consequence, the sense of reality of ancient religions, but also that of monotheistic religion, is based on the vision and experience of the cosmos as a continuous, uninterrupted background reality, something "truly real," possessing therefore an overpowering spiritual and cultural significance. Even when faith in God dislodges or modifies the evidences of nature and the psychic world, it is matter-of-factly assumed that superhuman and supernatural reality is the divine handiwork, a constitution of being, a prototype in the divine mind.

*   *   *

Let us return, inside this great continuum of the cosmos, to its birth and the birth of the gods, and also to the notion of reality as opposed to subjective experience. It becomes at once plausible that humanity, placed before the cosmic regularities and forces, conceives power in the human community as a derivative or replica of the cosmic power and order. The community then *must* be a privileged place, selected by the gods as their eminent domain. Order and power become inseparable as articulations of the structure of the real, and they are inseparable also from the story of the divine cosmic birth, which accounts for reality, permanence, and continuity. Not only is the community linked in obvious ways to a transcendental original, but so are the individual members of the collectivity: *through* the community they are linked to the transcendent. The reality of power becomes an individual's primary experience of the reality of the community and, beyond it, of the reality of the divine order.

Order and power emerge as fundamental features of communal reality, whether one understands the universe in which this occurs as organized by intramundane gods or created by an external agent. The birth, the composition, and the organization of the universe and the functioning rules prevailing in it are faithfully and exactly reflected in the origin, the human composition, the organizational outline, and the laws of the human community. Thus the first human collective already provides the first political experience.

This much we saw in general outline in Chapter One, where I also pointed out, mostly through architectural illustration, that just as in the realm of the sacred, so also in realm of the political, there are two worlds—the real (the divine, the archetypal, the ontologically necessary) and the copy (the human, the imitation, the contingent). The relationship between the two is, of course, all-important. Not only must the copy permanently conform to the original—and, if it does deviate, be brought back to the norm through appropriate ceremonies of atonement and reparation—it must also be ruled and governed in the spirit of and according to the letter of this relationship. The ancient view of the political community was a polity in close relation with the cosmos, therefore a unity guaranteed an absolute cohesion. Consequently, the ruler—king, emperor, tribal chief, or high priest—has always been extremely important because he stood for the principle and nucleus of politics. He was the living guarantee of the community's survival, which would be assured, even beyond his death, by appointed procedures that would maintain the dynasty. As the link between reality and its replica, the ruler was a sacred person who would trace the origin and source of his power not to the previous ruler but to the supreme deity from whom power in its uncorrupted nature was derived. This was true of the Egyptian pharaohs, who, by their epithet son of Ra, traced their authority to the sun god Ra; and it is also true of the pope, who is not, strictly speaking, considered a successor of the preceding pontiff but a direct successor of St. Peter.

The ruler's sacred character is vitally important. As far back as we can reach into history, the political community was both a church and a state, with one or the other aspect gaining temporary supremacy. Some peoples developed a theocratic constitution headed by a priest-king or a divine emperor who ruled a homogeneous mass. For some Indo-Europeans, according to the researches of Georges Dumézil, a tripartite division of functions was characteristic: a priestly caste secured the vital contact with the supernal powers; a warrior class was entrusted with defense and conquest; and a third, more indeterminate category, including peasants, traders, artisans, and foreigners, provided for the subsistence of all.[2] All these patterns of political organization and rule became sacralized, so that the state appears from the beginning as a hierophany, an expression of the sacred in its totality. One may conjecture that this is why citizens obeyed the coercive forms of the state's governing: mobilization for war, the imposition of justice, the enforcement of contracts, the preservation of tranquility, and the punishing power of laws. On the other hand, it may be no less true that the obedience of the citizens was naturally concomitant with the issuing of orders. The reality of politics was not a superimposed measure; it was born with humanity, and the articulation of functions, tripartite or otherwise, was implicit in the institutional requirements which gave expression to human nature.

2. See Dumézil's many works on linguistics, tribal structure, myths, and epic sagas of the entire Indo-European area from the Indus to the Tiber.

The notion that people "invented" politics to add to a preexisting "state of nature" is itself an invention of the formulators of the contract theory, from the Sophists to Hobbes and Rousseau. In fact, political power has an immediate fascination which takes its place in the domain of the *mysterium tremendum,* while its specific function is to transfer the sacred into the profane sphere. Better than the ancient temple, the ancient palace was able to articulate power, to turn it to a wide variety of concrete tasks from enforcing military service to levying taxes, controlling labor, and maintaining class stratification (recall the structure of the ideal society in Plato's *Republic*). It was able to do so precisely because it was located at the intersection of "high" and "low," and because it never let its celestial origin fade from the collective memory.

How could this memory of the community's divine origin—its primordial link with cosmic-divine reality—fade? All rituals pertaining to the community's foundation celebrated the political state and aimed at keeping it a permanent microcosm, by periodically purifying it and delivering it of its flaws, that is, its deviations from the model. In the king, all powers were concentrated, from the ceremonies surrounding his birth to, in some cases, the eventual sacred act of his murder or suicide.[3] But even if the person of the king died by ritual force, the figure of the ruler remained permanently the same. The successor was regarded merely as the rejuvenation of the old ruler. The king was considered provider, rainmaker, guarantor of fertility (for fields, cattle, and women—for which he provided through a sacral mating with the high-priestess), and also healer of specific diseases (the thaumaturgic kings of France were believed able to heal scrofula). He also embodied the community's cohesion, his presence squashing disorder. If civil war has universally been considered as the greatest misfortune that may befall a nation, it is because through such an internal conflict the king's body was seen to be pulled apart, a sacrilegious act.

The king, as is now obvious, is not an easily circumscribed figure as the source and transmitter of power. He concretizes

---

3. These practices were witnessed by seventeenth- and eighteenth-century European travelers in Malabar, on the southwestern coast of the Indian subcontinent.

power, and in this sense he embodies the community and is a symbol of its unity. His various functions do not clearly separate him from the priesthood (in prerevolutionary France the king was also an ordained priest). He is thus a mediator between the celestial sphere and this world,[4] a supreme judge like King Minos in the Hellenic underworld and St. Louis "under the oak tree." He guarantees the access of the community to the primordial state of being and is entrusted, as René Guénon writes, with the adjustment of the cosmic-divine message to the language of the multitudes. In this capacity he performs a quasi-divine revelation.[5] Let us bear in mind that in Christian sacred history too, royal figures, the Magi-Kings, perform this same function by revealing Christ's birth to the world. Moses and Buddha were also of royal origin, and Jesus himself was "from the House of David." It is appropriate, then, that kings should be the first to hear of the presence of one higher than they, proving their status in Christianity too as the mediators par excellence and witnesses of divine manifestation.

Different political communities applied the "religion of king and state" in different ways, according to the pertinent civilizational presuppositions. A characteristic feature of all royal myths, however, is the belief that the royal figures are themselves the *axis mundi,* and that their hieratic, rigid posture is the link between the transcendent and the sacred ground on which the community had its origin and lives out its destiny. The king of the Skilluk tribe in what is now the Sudan is untouchable, above-earthly; even his spittle, an inner substance in most archaic religions, may not touch the ground. He must always be in a flawless physical state, for his well-being symbolizes and guarantees that of his people. Should he fall ill, he would be discarded, and another healthy specimen elected, as "powerful and just" as his predecessor. Clearly, the powers above cannot be faulted about the mediator they choose. The same principle prevails in Tibet, where continuity is secured through the choice, at the moment of the Dalai Lama's death, of a

4. Note the similarity between the Hebrew *Melech,* "king," and *Malech,* "angel."

5. Guénon, *Le Roi du monde* (Paris: Éditions Traditionnelles, 1939), 38.

newborn baby believed to possess sacred characteristics by transfusion from the old spiritual head. The ruler is both sacred and profane, the visible face of the divinity, just as the divinity is the invisible source of the ruler's power. This double reality constitutes the ruler's sphere of power; it is the supreme manifestation of the community. In consequence, the king is charged with a tremendous responsibility: not only must he perform many functions, but he must do so with a ritual precision. As a hieratic figure he is a closely controlled mechanism, for any deviation from the cosmic pattern that he represents here below would plunge the body politic into nonbeing, a concept related to what Christians call sin.

Some illustrations should cast light on the king's embodiment of the power of the state and the state's embodiment of an original reality, the community's supreme reference point. In traditional societies, politics in the modern sense does not exist, writes Jean Hani.[6] The central actor is neither the government nor the legislator—both are embedded in the life of the universe which has its own time and rhythm. Thus the act of governing does not follow actual, day-by-day needs and operations. It is rather a dependency of religion, and it plays out the model which is interpreted by authorities competent in the movements of the cosmos. In China, the emperor was understood to occupy the center (as China itself was called the "empire of the center") from which, in Hani's words, he governed "the four orients, separated the two principles, Yin and Yang, determined the four seasons, balanced the five elements, and set the astronomical calculations." In other words, he was not a mundane ruler but a cosmocrator, symbolized also by the fact that as mediator between heaven and earth he wore a round hat and a square-shaped skirt, the shapes of the mandala.

The same is true of other ancient rulers, up to and beyond the Western Middle Ages and in premodern Japan, Africa, and most of Asia. Whether in Persia or Egypt, the function of ruling supposed divine attributes which demanded that the ruler extend his power over his territory as the *imago mundi,* the "image of the world," an image further represented by the capital and the royal palace. The gradual compacting of power is also its ultimate force

6. Hani, *La Royauté sacrée, Du pharaon au roi très chrétien* (Paris: Éditions Trédaniel, 1984), 60.

and majesty. As we approach the ruler's person, everything in his proximity—the apparel he wears, the objects he handles, the way he travels—all bear the signs and symbols of rule, sovereignty, and sacredness.[7] This is because all these things have a divine prototype; all refer back from their this-worldly materiality to what we called "real reality" as it exists in more majesty, in greater concentration, and closer to the ultimate source of power. In this domain, nothing is left to chance or even to the ruler's whim. We have mentioned that Romulus, in founding Rome, ploughed a trench around the site of the future city and lifted his plough each time he reached the future location of gates in the wall. There is a symbolism at work in this act: while the walls symbolize the state and are inviolable, the gates are open to foreigners, traders, and daily traffic. The ground here is not sacred. Foreign delegations, the potential enemy and the representatives of alien gods, will pass through. Similarly, the active life of the common citizenry shows little direct signs of the sacred. Only as the sovereign and the marks of sovereignty are approached do persons and objects become endowed with a surplus existence, expressed in the sacred.

On high ceremonial occasions, for example, the Holy Roman emperor Henry II wore a mantle which represented the firmament with the constellations and the signs of the zodiac. This signified the emperor's sacred power and his role as mediator between the forces sustaining the cosmos and his own people. The mantle itself was a sign, a magic object. Another example is Charlemagne's chapel at Aix-la-Chappelle, a copy of the church of San Vitale in Ravenna and thus linked to the Roman empire, the source of the Frankish king's power. The chapel embodies a number of symbols. It is octagonal since the octagon represents the fusion of the earth and heaven. Thus the chapel is no mere container of the emperor's devotion but like Henry's mantle is a sign, a sign of eternity. Another sophisticated symbol is the Abbey of Saint-Denis near Paris, the burial place of kings. The abbey was the concep-

---

7. In South America under Spanish rule, territorial governors at assembly time would greet the king's hat which was presiding. This act of obeisance did not prevent the assemblies of the notables from disagreeing with the officers representing the king of Spain, however.

tion of Abbot Suger, inspirer of the cathedrals, and it served to interpret in stone, glass, and light an increasingly ethereal gradation, the theology of Pseudo-Dionysius the Areopagite (who was identified, falsely, with Saint Denis, the first bishop of Paris), centered around the "nameless God" who could not be conceptualized. At the same time, it was also the symbol of the elevation of the senses, a conscious refutation of the contemporary heretical sects' exclusive stress on spirituality. As Suger explained in the dedicatory document, obviously aiming his words at the heretics' Manichaean contempt for matter: "What radiates inside [the church] is announced by the gilded gates. . . . With the aid of sensory beauty the soul rises to the true beauty, and from the earth where the soul lay prostrate, she comes to heavenly life through the light of these splendors."[8]

These illustrations indicate the sacrality of power in the persons of rulers and in the objects, buildings, and cities which surround them in their exercise of power. They cannot fulfill their profane function without being replenished, so to speak, from above. The communion between the two levels make it clear that politics and religion are inseparable and were always so regarded. Julien Ries mentions the Brahman-rajah of India and the flamen-rex in Rome who "constitute two halves of a single organism, that of sovereignty."[9] It is characteristic of the careful delineation of divine and earthly powers that the *flamen* was not permitted to sleep outside Rome for fear that he might displace the sacred and leave the state unprotected. On the other hand, he was not to set eyes on the army since, as a sacred personage, he carried not only

8. Quoted in Georges Duby, *Le Temps des cathédrales, l'art et la société 980–1420* (Paris: Gallimard, 1976). Suger further explained, "Those who criticize us [for this worldly magnificence] hold that a saintly soul, an unsoiled mind, a faithful intention are sufficient for holy celebration. We certainly admit that these are essentials. But we assert also that one must serve [the holy sacrifice] with the external ornaments of the sacred receptacles: to inner purity there corresponds the nobility of external forms." Suger, *De rebus in administratione sua gestis,* quoted in Erwin Panofsky's *Abbot Suger* (Princeton: Princeton University Press, 1979), 67.

9. Both Brahman-rajah and flamen-rex are quite literally "priest-rulers." See Julien Ries, *Les chemins du sacré dans l'histoire* (Paris: Aubier, 1985), 95, 141.

the power of protection but also that of curse: the arms would have been polluted at his contact.[10]

Examples abound of power which is efficacious only when sacralized. In ancient Israel, Samuel forged a nation out of the tribes by calling them together and telling them of Saul's divine approval: he was "the Lord's chosen one." Solomon's power was sacralized as he built the temple, sacrificed in it, and blessed the people. In Sumer, the king was both head of state and high priest, thus integrating temple and palace. Nor was this universal concept abolished by Christianity. Gregory of Nazianzus, describing the burial of emperor Constantius II commented that the emperor's body "takes the road towards the Apostles' glorious temple which holds the sacred race of the Caesars whose merits equal those of the Apostles and of Christ." Further, throughout Byzantine history, the emperors never ceased negotiating with the church for a closer integration of church and state power. This policy, described as "caesaropapism," in fact stood on ancient biblical grounds: the fuller reinforcement of royal power by the prophetic power, with the ultimate source of authority in the divine.

This conception of the royal figure has been continuous from the most ancient times to our own, and it was only modified, not rejected, by Christianity. Yet in the latter's vision, the view of the cosmos as a supreme but magically manipulable model could find no place. Christian "desacralization" of the heavens resulted in the assumption, gradually demonstrated by the investigations of science, that there are no intermediate beings, forces, and spirits between God, the universe, and human beings— at least not in the sense of a cosmic model to be copied by a mundane replica. As early as in the Hellenistic-Roman culture of the second and third centuries, both Christianity and pagan thought (at least in its Stoic forms) began to posit a *moral model* of the world. For Christians, this model was set down in the Gospels; for pagans it was rooted

---

10. This interdict may have been a consequence of the separation of functions in the tripartite system: the class of priests and the class of warriors cooperated but were always distinct. Compare this heritage with India's caste system, with its much greater divisions. Indeed, the word for caste in Hindi, *varna,* means "individual nature," that is, selection, difference, differentiation.

in Stoic and Neoplatonic wisdom. A quasi-material cosmos as a source of divine-magic emanations as well as an object of magic manipulation was no longer imaginable. Political rule adjusted itself to a moral ideal, setting its vision not on a divine cosmology but on the "ideal republic." Marcus Aurelius, for example, although he conformed with some reluctance to the hieratic status he occupied, had an essentially moral (Stoic) concept of his place as the head of an empire he knew was declining.

This does not, however, mean the eclipse of the ruler as a sacred figure. Marcus Aurelius had the misfortune of ruling a community that no longer believed in its own mission, a mission last formulated, at least for the cultured public, by Virgil more than two centuries before. The emperor was now placed between a self-doubting paganism and the Christian believers awaiting their historic role. In fact, Christianity endowed the ruler with a vigorous new sacred, although it was more difficult to work out than any pre-Christian system of power. It was to be the task of many centuries.

The Christian concept of the sacred naturally affected the political sphere in important ways. I have mentioned the continuity implicit in the ancient worldview: it rested on the correspondence of all parts of the cosmos, on the reflection of the macrocosm in the microcosm, on the magic-manipulative potency of the latter on the former, on the reflection of the primordial model in the human replica. We saw that this mighty image was discarded by the nascent Christian religion, although the process of elimination proved to be many centuries long. In the place of the static and immobile cosmic—thus *spatial*—reality, Christianity introduced a *conceptual* division between divine and human and, in the divinity itself, a separation between God as transcendent and God as personal, a separation vividly emphasized in the Incarnation. Through the Incarnation God became a personal model to be imitated and followed, while at the same time he remained absolutely transcendent. The cosmic model used to be a self-contained archetype, a changeless reality; through Christ, the Christian God became a dynamic force, finishing the work of creation with the help of humanity. An open future, a *history,* replaced the routine conformity to the celestial model because the Christ of history represented and demanded active participation from all.

In the ancient view, the gods (always belonging to a specific human community, never universal) gave their favor to one territory, one nation, or one empire, since they themselves were bound to one place. The Christian God, in contrast, extended his rule to all humanity; moreover his "kingdom was not of this world," it was a moral dominion. No nation could thus claim to be *the* replica of the divine order; nations could only try to capture God's blessing and benevolence in the moral order, through moral obedience. Humanity's spiritual powers were thus released and mobilized instead of being tied to a sacralized political order like the Confucian state or the Indian caste system.

Christianity retained many pre-Christian notions, ideas, and ritual practices, though. Just one illustration: the meticulousness of pagan ceremonies was intended to bend the gods' favor to the interests of the community, since the pagans believed that the cosmic model had to be reproduced and the peaceful or turbulent expressions of its forces reenacted. Pagan rituals were mechanically precise, and so, eventually, were the rituals of Christianity: the celebrant's gestures at the altar during the Mass, the reconsecration of profanized holy places, the formulas in the confession of sin or in exorcism. In other words, Christianity too observes the immemorial rules of sacrality; it too knows the meaning of deviations from a higher pattern and atonement for them. The substantial difference lies in the displacement of the sacred from the cosmos to the morally focused relationship between God and humanity. This is the risk Christianity takes, and this provides the nostalgia many ages and peoples have felt for the immobile cosmos and its precise imitation. To be sure, the moral relationship has the divine being as its center, but the divine being calls forth an endlessly improvable approach to his will. The *imitatio Christi* is never complete; it must always be further perfected. This challenge to the human will energizes individual life and history, but it does not guarantee that God will remain in focus.

When translated into political terms, the Christian concept of the sacred inevitably comes to emphasize the dynamic, moral component of political rule. As I said before, the ritual aspect remains firmly in place; the center of gravity, however, is concentrated in the moral content of one's action, and without the moral content the acts themselves seem to run empty and contrary to God's plans for humanity. The church's ceremonial life thus tends toward supporting both the sacralization and the moralization of the community and the ruler. But this sacralization is a mere wish and hope instead of the certitude that the ancient celebrant possessed after the ritual had been performed according to prescriptions. The margin left between ritual sacralization and effective sacralization—in a way the margin between human performance and the standard set by Christ in the Incarnation—puts a question mark on the effectiveness of the sacred.[11]

The adoption of the Christian religion by emperor Constantine (a mere century and a half after Marcus Aurelius) was to change power relationships in the late-Roman and post-Roman world. Under Christ's kingship, the strong "imperial" personalities who now emerged were no longer the emperors, whose role as Christian leaders of an empire still structured by pagan notions was only a little less ambiguous than Marcus Aurelius's. Rather the strong personalities were prelates, popes, bishops, and holy men: Ambrose, Augustine, Jerome, Anthony, Gregory, Leo, and many others. No wonder that imperial and other official prerogatives— as well as the symbolic elements of protocol and apparel—passed from the state's officers to the bishops. This evolution heralded the reinforcement of the sacred component of political power, the supremacy sought by the church over the state expressed in Pope Galasius's teaching about the "two swords" (A.D. 494). In essence, this teaching was that God entrusted pope and emperor with rule over Christians, but that the spiritual authority of the first was superior to the temporal power of the second; before God's tribunal, the pope was responsible also for the emperor's soul, thus for his management of the community.

The image of the church as an absolute monarchy with roots

11. The church is aware of this "margin" and that it has often been the cause of radical criticism: since only morality should confer consecration, should not all churchmen be morally good? The answer is found in the general moral imperfection of humanity. Yet the sacraments are valid, the church teaches, even though the consecrator may be in a state of sin. The sacrament is valid per se; its validity does not depend on the priest's moral state.

in heaven gradually imprinted itself on the mostly Germanic kingdoms in which originally the tribal chieftain had been "first among
equals." This "regal pontificalism," as Ernst Kantorowitz calls the
end product of the historical process, rests on the belief that
government is a *mysterium* entrusted to the king who is also a high
priest. Melchizedek and Solomon, the Roman *pontifex* ("high
priest") and the "august" Caesars, and also St. Peter provide a continuous line pointing in this direction. Thus actions accomplished
in the name of these state mysteries were considered as valid as
sacraments; that is, their validity was considered independent of
the personal merit of the performer.

This was, in brief, the Christian version of the ruler's sacralization. While the pagan-Roman element is not to be underesti-
mated, the main justification derives from ecclesiastical thinking.
Kantorowicz calls it the "clericalization of royal function" and
speaks of jurists searching for formulas of royal rule "similar to
those of the Mass."[12] By the fourteenth century the doctrine
reached a formulation that could hardly be improved. In the words
of Lucas of Parma, "In the same way as men are united spiritually
in the spiritual body whose Christ is head . . . they are also morally
and spiritually united in the body of the republic whose head is the
Prince." Reality was closely accompanied by symbolization: the
pope adorned his tiara with a golden crown, donned the imperial
purple, and was preceded by the imperial banners when he rode
through the streets of Rome. The emperor wore under his crown
a mitre, donned the pontifical shoes and other clerical raiments,
and received, like a bishop, the ring at his coronation.

It would be an error to see in these developments a uniquely
Christian line of thought. To be sure, Christianity had imprinted
its own powerful doctrinal system on matters outside the church
and theology, yet in doing so it merely recalled ancient and pre-
Christian operative principles. By virtue of Christ's words "Ren-
der . . . to Caesar the things that are Caesar's" the sacralization of
the Christian ruler was a cause won in advance. Some also pointed
out in an attempt to legitimize temporal rulers that empires had

12. See Kantorowicz, *The King's Two Bodies: A Study in Medieval
Political Theology* (Princeton: Princeton University Press, 1957).

existed long before the Incarnation (an argument much used by the jurists of Frederick II and those of the French kings). In spite of the conflicts and ambiguities from the beginning between church and state (for example those between Ambrose and Theodosius, between the papacy and Constantinople, Gregory VII and the German emperors, Boniface VIII and the king of France), the two powers offered mutual support as both were spiritually shaped by the acknowledgement of the sacred.

While this was essentially the same sacred as that acknowledged by the ancients, recall that the ancient conception saw a static sacred which needed only to be exactly reproduced and re-enacted. The Christian conception, in contrast, was of a personal God who could not be duplicated but whose moral demands were to be followed under penalty of exclusion from the community formed around the Incarnation. The Christian model of the sacred was thus a *moral* model, as dynamic as the human beings who carry out the divine commandments.

*   *   *

What is behind the divinely ordained political power, whether in pagan or Christian empires? Marcel Gauchet states it is always assumed that the power holder fulfills a mediating function between the "soul of the world" and the human order.[13] Christianity has emphasized this link even more than ancient religion did. For Christianity, the true mediator is not merely a correspondence between divine macrocosm and worldly microcosm but rather the person of Christ himself, his two natures joined in one body, so that he is the true ruler, the true king.[14] The worldly king, by imitating Christ *morally,* had the sacred imprinted on him, but it was imprinted in

13. Marcel Gauchet, *Le désenchantement du monde, Une histoire politique de la religion* (Paris: Gallimard, 1985), 143.

14. Later medieval sects, considered by church and state as heretical and subversive, made much of this point. Bending the argument to themselves, they wanted to establish a community, more church than state, more spiritual than power wielding, in which Christ alone would be recognized as ruler, in which only his preaching of love would be acknowledged as "law." This led to a theocracy cemented by "love" alone, obviously a fragile basis for a community of human beings, all of them interpreting love in their own subjective and emotional way.

such a way that it could be lost again: the ruler had again and again to deserve it through moral acts. Let me emphasize the point. While the ancients' conformity to the cosmic model requires meticulous attitudes and performances, conformity to Christ's kingship is based primarily on the moral grounds implicit in the Incarnation. Once these grounds are established, power becomes sacralized.

There are writers who stress the separation of palace and temple in ancient times and of state and church in modern times, quoting Jesus as the source of the modern distinction between the domains of Caesar and God. It seems to me that these writers underestimate the true aspects of power and order, as well as the undeniable fact of their necessary interaction. Everything I have said so far may serve as a demonstration that the use of *power,* that is, the direction and maintenance of human beings as a community, presupposes an *order,* understood as antedating the community, which gives it its origin, directives, meaning, and cohesion. The established worldly order stands in need of power—in the first place to remind citizens of their conformity to the model and in the second place to preserve its structures which are imprints of the superior reality. It follows that order and power are intertwined, and that their dual manifestation appears wherever a community exists as "church" and "state," as spiritual order and temporal power. The whole modern political problematic has its roots here: Must order be derived from a cosmic model and a set of moral imperatives guaranteed by a divine figure, or are there valid substitutes for them? If so, are these substitutes credible enough to legitimize the power derived from them?

As order justifies and legitimizes power, a myth comes into existence, translating the reality of order into the operational discourse of power. The myth must be evident and vigorous, so that we do not question the reality of order behind it. The king's "two bodies" thus become meaningful: power emanates from a concretely perceived, physical being (and is channeled through his executors), but it is substantiated by the "invisible body" enveloped in the myth.

The crucial problem of political power, at all times but especially in ours, is that myths change, leaving the reality of order difficult to locate. In other words, myth is not seen as a myth but is allowed only a derivative status of reality. A community which begins to doubt whether its political order and its manifestations of power have any ontological status has begun gliding toward anarchy and unguided change. When various thinkers and historians speak of vast historical and cultural crises—Paul Hazard dates one such around 1715, and Oswald Spengler locates one two hundred years later—there is, in the back of their diagnoses, the recognition that a new age has been entered that no longer supports the accustomed public attitudes and postulates. The crisis is not merely the failure of the "transmission system"; it is not that the old myth is no longer working to transmit the accepted order. Rather, the crisis is that history is in labor with a wholly new myth transmitting a new order that makes the old superfluous.

It is an intriguing question whether our age is capable of generating a myth with the power to move nations and civilizations. The question is not whether we have the will or the ingenious formulas to do so but whether our orientation to myth even makes it possible. The ancient concept of order, power, and myth faded during the first centuries of Christianity, and many today believe that the Christian concept too is losing its own credibility, even in areas where officially it is still operative. But the question again is not whether a new myth or a new understanding of power is taking shape under our eyes but whether contemporary Western people are even able to make and accept myths. Do we still possess mythopoeic faculties that can shape a reality that we cannot know except through the mediation of a (political) myth? In short, is power still sacralized in the Christian milieu?

Such questions may only be answered by an entire civilization which engenders and gives form to the fundamentals of thought, sentiment, and judgment. No individual can succeed at such a task, and certainly not outside his own cultural and political context. Sacred manifestations and political myths are generated at the level of vast communities, and then only on condition that the surrounding civilizational postulates are favorable to such a birth, something we can perceive only in retrospect.

In traditional cultures, including those infused with Christianity, the perception of political power was conditioned by the action of "high" and "low," the first endowing the second with meaning and giving it a structure according to its own higher primordial structure. If the higher (heaven in Christianity, Olympus for the Greeks, or the empire of light for Zoroastrians, for example) constitutes a hierarchy, then the human realm too is ordered on this model. Political power may thus be understood as a descent of light, of wisdom, or of absolute knowledge. A conception of such a descent of light along hierarchical lines was supplied to early Christian and then medieval times by Plotinian philosophy, itself derived from that of Plato and Pythagoras. This conception saw everything in the universe as a series of deescalating emanations from the One (not otherwise namable), each further degree of descent losing some of the original light and essence, thus approaching darkness. The end of the universe in Plotinus's system was to be the reabsorption of all the multiplicities, each more deficient than the previous one in the hierarchy, into the One.

The link between Plotinus and medieval theology, and even more explicitly between Plotinus and medieval political thought, was the speculative system of Pseudo-Dionysius the Areopagite (probably of the sixth century), who "Christianized" Neoplatonic thought as a "celestial hierarchy," articulating it with great precision and deriving from it an "ecclesiastical hierarchy." The concepts elaborated by Pseudo-Dionysius, and already by Plotinus, were applicable to mundane hierarchies as well, among them the political one. The ancient systems, writes René Roques, one of Pseudo-Dionysius's modern commentators, were philosophies of order. The soul, the state, the societies of intellectual discourse were all supposed to reproduce, in their particular ways, the order presented to them by the universe. To accept the hierarchical order was the equivalent of carrying out the divine law.[15] Pseudo-Dionysius brought important modifications to Plotinus's view, though. While the latter stressed the moments of emanation and the terminal reabsorption, a kind of immense breathing of the universe, the former, a Christian thinker, emphasized the idea of divine grace. This allows a freer relationship between the transcendent and the

15. René Roques, *L'univers dionysien, Structure hiérarchique du monde selon le Pseudo-Denys* (Paris: Éditions du Cerf, 1983), 35, 39.

hierarchies, providing opportunity for concrete historical developments and changes. Yet Pseudo-Dionysius remained in the line of Plato. He saw hierarchy as the true framework of political power, for it expresses the ideal of power: the distinction of social classes, their cohesion in the spirit of justice, and the perfect adjustment of individuals and classes to their own particular function.

We observe that in Greek, Roman, and Christian civilizations, from the time of the *Iliad* to the doctrine of absolute monarchy, political power was conceived as the articulation and transmission of an *essence* through the levels of hierarchy.[16] One might say that, by making this evident, Pseudo-Dionysius formulated a Christian cosmology, equivalent to although different from ancient cosmologies. Pseudo-Dionysius's model was less explicit than Augustine's City of God, yet it was eminently useful both for the state and for illuminating a Christian civilization. It survived for centuries and would have been operative for a longer time if Pseudo-Dionysius had not been identified, justifiably, with the Platonic school in Christendom over against the Aristotelian school, which later attracted the most important loyalties. Even so, Abbot Suger of Saint-Denis drew from him his own artistic inspiration, and St. Thomas gives him a favorable and admiring testimony.

Pseudo-Dionysius's worldview was the crowning statement of sacralized power in Christendom. He did not speak of politics directly, but politics was implicit in his conception and minute description of the hierarchies. He drew a clear line between his own thought and the two popular worldviews of his time, the Stoic and the Neoplatonic, of which the former proposed a self-contained eternal cosmos and the latter posited an inaccessible One and a sequence of increasing degradation. Extricating himself from both *idées reçues* (roughly, "transmitted ideas"), Pseudo-Dionysius taught that reality is constructed from the highest down, and between higher and lower there are intermediaries, receiving and transmitting the sacred realities. These divine realities reveal

16. Absolute monarchy contradicted the Plotinian–Pseudo-Dionysian conception insofar as it denied in principle the intermediate gradations between high and low and placed all power in the hands of the king. Thus this doctrine abolished the hierarchy through which power descends and ascends.

themselves progressively, and their self-explication in the temporal order is the source of new insights, of a new comprehension, a new science. One might say without exaggeration that Pseudo-Dionysius's system contains the thesis of Cardinal Newman, twelve hundred years in advance. This system does not end in the Plotinian impasse, that is, the reabsorption of a world whose existence is at the end revealed as unjustified. Before the world of the Christian ends in beatitude, it has made room for new modalities of the contingent and even the transitory.[17]

At every point, the Christian sacralization proved to be adaptive, even in comparison with the other speculative systems and doctrines of the cosmos, including Stoicism, Neoplatonism, and Gnosticism. Yet despite its accommodation of change, Christianity suggested a political sacralization similar to the ancient: the building of the City of God in the service of civilization. But the Christian sacralization never meant to serve one civilization alone. Even Augustine's somber perspective allows for the intermingling of good and evil, for a history that extends indefinitely, and thus for a wide field for the new. He stood before the perspective of history as he stood before the Mediterranean landscape: I know, he wrote, that Nature has fallen from divine grace, but, O God, how beautiful it is even in this fallen state! So with history: the struggle between good and evil exposes nations and civilizations to great risks, but because the church possesses Christ's promise, it will forever offer the sacred model to the human endeavor.

It is the subject of a perhaps never-ending controversy whether the church has proved to be true to the Augustinian and Pseudo-Dionysian schema, or whether, as critics hold, it has allowed the sacred model to be dissolved in the vicissitudes of the historic civilizations it has sponsored. We gave a prudent answer to this question when we suggested that Christianity detached itself from the cosmos and that its hierarchies separated themselves from the last manifestation of the static hierarchy introduced by Plotinus.

This is a lasting controversy because it turns around the Incarnation and its political interpretations. The majority of patristic texts make clear that the royalty exercised by Jesus while he was

17. René Roques, *L'univers dionysien,* 124.

a man on earth was purely spiritual. After all, Jesus himself in-
directly recognized the Roman empire. Yet even at the end of the
sixteenth century, to say nothing of earlier times, a strong-willed
pope like Sixtus V claimed temporal authority on the ground that
Jesus possessed it.[18] Sixtus's claim, refuted by Cardinal Bellarmine among others, was a swan song of the historical papal claims
to temporal rule, the last vestige of sacralized power within
Christendom. At about the same time, Jean Bodin in France and
James I in England were elaborating the doctrine of absolute
monarchy, leaning once more on the divine right of kings. The
formulas asserting divine right remained steady references for
about another three centuries but became increasingly empty of
content. The sacred model behind them faded because the human
side of Christ in the Incarnation was emphasized more and more,
first by humanism, then by the Reformation, until finally in the
seventeenth century science made the whole debate irrelevant. A
new cosmology had come into existence, and it caught people's
imagination.

18. See James Brodrick, S. J., *Robert Bellarmine* (London: Burns and
Oates, 1961), 108-9.

CHAPTER THREE

Desacralized Vision

Chapter Two led to the conclusion that while the sacred continues to be effective throughout humanity's existence, it may change its shape and mode of expression from one civilization to another, from one cultural context to the next. Recognizing the fact of sacralization's change, however, may not bring us any closer to a grasp of its actual meaning. All epochs have known the sacralization of power, but in each different time it assumed different aspects and depended on changing postulates. Christopher Dawson, in the very first paragraph of his book *Christianity and the New Age* introduces this problem of civilizational and cultural transformation. For centuries, Dawson writes, a civilization may follow the same path, worshiping the same gods, cherishing the same ideals, acknowledging the same moral and intellectual standards. Then all at once a change will come, the springs of the old life run dry, and people suddenly awake to a new world in which the ruling principles of the former age seem to have lost their validity and to have become inapplicable and meaningless.[1]

Dawson does not claim to know what causes the transformation, nor do the other scholars and thinkers who have studied history's decisive junctures in ancient and modern times, including Polybius, Augustine, Giambattista Vico, and Oswald Spengler. One can really only propose proximate causes, then search for the

1. Dawson, *Christianity and the New Age* (Manchester, N.H.: Sophia Institute Press, 1985), 1.

47

circumstances and the consequences of change. This search must be rooted in what is specific and unique about a civilization; it must probe the culture's relationship with the sacred as the latter articulates itself according to a view of the world, the cosmos, and the cosmic laws. The fundamental questions every civilization asks, and perseveres in asking, are How were the gods born? Why did they fashion the world as they did? and What are the consequences for humanity and the human community?

The answers to these questions constitute a compact body of knowledge or belief that requires total devotion and cooperation on the part of the members of the community. All the members of the community, especially king and clergy, the appointed spokesmen, as well as the permanently expressive and revered symbols, acts, and consecrated words—indeed, the entire sacred apparatus—are united with the high verities, translating them into important factors of existence: politics, art, science, education, law, and social institutions.

Many influential thinkers contend that from the image of the cosmos that presided over all past civilizations and was held sacred and immutable by traditional wisdom there split off a specifically Western image, contary to that tradition. We saw in Chapters One and Two that the ancient and pre-Christian cosmic image was permanent and stable, that it merely had to be interpreted by special people for its laws to be perceived as operative within the community. In Christianity, however, there is a radically different view of the cosmos and humanity's relationship to it. There is suddenly no cosmos full of vital elements—gods, spirits, and daemons—but a universe empty of influences, correspondences, and magic manipulations with one God at its center who created everything and whose knowledge and power grasps all things. Moreover, this God chose a particular moment in the history of a particular people to send his Son as an incarnate God, a sacred person, to assume fully the human condition, to live among other human beings, and to die in their full view. While some argue that every religious system has its own incarnation myth and that gods in various mythologies, from Krishna to Dionysus to Horus, mingle with humanity only to reascend the celestial ladder, all these other myths differ in one important respect from the Christian account of the Incarnation. Only in Christianity does God become his own sole mediator and exclusive guarantor of the sacred relationship. There is henceforth no room for special messengers, personified forces, or mythical heroes who strive for or against God's will, as was the case in the Olympian pantheon. Nor is there room for Gnosticism's elaborate postulations of an evil world created by the demiurgos and of a God reduced to impotence.

In vivid contrast to the cosmic avatars of other systems, Christ was actually seen by his contemporaries. They could hold reasoned conversations with him and could witness his acts and later his suffering and passion. The consequences of the Christian Incarnation were far-reaching: through it God not only descended among human beings, he also lifted them up to him, establishing in and outside the church the conditions of mutual cooperation, "co-creation." The Incarnation also abolished the pagan view of time as an endlessly recurring cycle to which even the gods were subordinate. In its place was introduced the linear view of time in which acts and events could occur only once; they could never occur again. St. Augustine castigated the old notion of pagan speculation, strongly rooted even in his own time, telling Christians that recurring time cycles would mean that the Incarnation and Resurrection would happen over and over again without end. The new conception places a far greater burden on the human agent. No one can claim powerlessness in the grip of an endless cycle of events; rather all are now to some extent shapers of the time in which they live. This has led in many cases to the claim of a self-divinized status by enthusiasts and false prophets, and it also leads generally to the notion that with God's guarantee—and even without it—human beings may become sole masters of their own destiny.

Whatever we may think of the vast changes brought about by the Christian vision of God, the universe, and humanity, it is evident that it has introduced a new civilizational image. Yet it is hard to speak, as Dawson did, of suddenness, since the fading traditions of the past still extend numerous influences into the new configuration, and the new in turn affects our comprehension of the past. Nor are all changes simultaneous, of course. Some elements of the past have a greater power of survival, or perhaps just inertia, while

others give way to the new garb more impatiently. Although it is
not easy to assign precise limits on the appearance of a new civilization, the outlines of change may yet be traceable if we focus
on a particular phenomenon—the desacralization of the Western
Christian vision, a process that can be examined through the paths
of science, art, and the concept of power.[2]

*   *   *

We are particularly concerned in this section with the fading of the
old cosmology and the rise of the new. Just as the ancient view of
the cosmos decisively influenced art, science, and the community's self-image, so does modern cosmology affect our civilization.
I noted how the concept of time changed from cyclical to linear,
bringing with it a number of weighty consequences. Human action
became unique, nonrepeatable, and not purifiable through subsequent existences (the doctrine of metempsychosis, widespread
in the ancient worldview). Human life now took upon itself the burden of full responsibility. Time itself lost its awesomeness, its non-
createdness.[3] In the Christian vision time is regarded as God's creation to be used by humanity as we also use other works of creation.
Time is now also the medium for the unrolling of the Christian
drama: it encloses *Heilsgeschichte,* the history of salvation, stretch-
ing from the expulsion from the Garden of Eden through the Incarnation to the final consummation as sin is overcome.

In the traditional view, space was as immobile as time. That
is, what movement there was in space was not toward any universal end or goal; movement did not mark any general progress.
Rather, objects moved toward their own natural place, their own
place of rest. Was this not obvious to common sense? Objects fell
on the ground, planets and stars described circles around the earth,
and the earth itself remained immobile, having no reason to move.
Such a worldview, still that of Aristotle, was not only at once

2. I will discuss science and art in this chapter, the concept of power in
Chapter Four.
3. Passages in ancient mythology that talk about the gods creating time
usually recount the creation of the sun, the moon, and the stars—that is, the
distribution of light and darkness. The full reality of time is not usually
tackled.

graspable by experience, it was also "human." In spite of the picture's immensity, it was still finite. It existed on a human scale, accessible to imagination and conceptualization.

Within this static milieu the movement of bodies could be nothing but a pseudo-movement, a succession of immobilities. The Stoic Zeno of Elea, for example, described the flight of an arrow, which, no matter how swiftly it flew from point A to point B, still had to remain in effect immobile. Since on its course the arrow had to occupy every intermediate position, and since an object cannot be moving when it occupies a position, the arrow must in fact always be at rest. In this regard, Anneliese Maier writes, motion "was identified at each particular moment with the state (terminus) attained at that moment. . . . so that motion was equal to the sum of all the states occupied. Thus the ontological definition of motion requires only the object that moves and the fact that the various termini are traversed in succession."[4] It follows that, since motion was not regarded as something distinct from the moving object and the states it occupies, nothing real corresponds to the concept of motion: it is a mere word.

Immobility was the privileged state of all objects, just as it was the state of the cosmic model. We may reverse the proposition: given that the cosmic model was immutable, things here below— objects and also empires—also preferred and tended to a state of rest. Since the cosmic model provides no paradigm for change, it could be understood only as a revolution, a violent motion contrary to nature to be quieted and resolved as soon as possible. To be sure, change in the world was acknowledged by the traditional worldview, but it was understood as the passage from the potential to the actual (see Aristotle's *Metaphysics* for the classical formulation). In fact, this means that no real change occurs, since the potential already contains the later, fully developed actual state. A consequence of a static space and motion is that time too is circular, forever returning on itself. What appears to be change is merely a return to something that has occurred before—no real change at all.

4. Maier, *On the Threshold of Exact Science,* ed. and introduced by Steven D. Sargent (Philadelphia: University of Pennsylvania Press, 1982), 30.

There was of course some opposition to the static cosmos even before Aristotle. Democritus and Epicurus, materialists both, saw the heavens and the stars as no more nor less alive than the rest of the material world. They did not believe, as their contemporaries did, that they were moved in their orbits by godlike beings. Yet their conception of an already desacralized universe ruled by chance and by a rudimentary atomic mechanics had no impact on the generally held worldview. Against them one could always explain movement in the otherwise immutable sphere of the celestial bodies from the cyclical view of time and circular uniform motion.[5] Change could then occur without anything new happening. Change was not the nature of things but something to be overcome on the search for the unchanging ideal. The Neoplatonist Proclus even compared the act of thinking to a sphere turning upon itself, a conception that recalls the statement of the Chaldean oracles that "all Sources and Principles describe an incessant circular movement."[6]

The idea of ultimate immobility, with its variants, is clearly deeply inscribed in the human vision. The place toward which movement tends and the circular movement itself are archetypes that we try to reproduce in this imperfect, restless world. For example, in Georges Duby's description of the circular movement in the processions of Clunyite monks, we at once grasp the interaction of the otherworldly model, this-worldly architectural design, and the discipline to which members of the monastery submitted themselves. "At Cluny . . . the community, praying with one voice, was moving ritually. It was like a very slow dance, translating the old myth of deliverance; it was the crossing of the Red Sea by the Hebrews, that of the desert; it was the slow progression of the dead Jesus towards his resurrection; the march of all men among the snares of this world. . . ."[7] In another passage,

5. Through the ages, the circle was one of the principal symbols of wisdom, the eternal recurrence of the same, the identity of beginning and end, perfection. It was symbolized by the serpent biting its own tail and by the caduceus, two intertwined serpents on the staff of Hippocrates.

6. Henry Corbin, *Le paradoxe du monothéisme* (Paris: Éditions de l'Herne, 1981), 60.

7. Duby, *Saint Bernard—l'Art cistercien* (Paris: Éditions Flammarion,

Duby mentions that the monastery's architecture served to situate the place in the *axis mundi,* the paradigm of rest, sacralized as the archetypal space for the earthly pilgrim's ambulation. The courtyard of the cloister, he notes, was "a square, coordinated at the four cardinal points, thus tearing away an ordered segment from cosmic unruliness."[8]

We must emphasize that although Christianity had laid the foundations for a new vision of the cosmos, the vision matured slowly, and Christianity was well integrated with the traditional view for quite a few centuries. (Later I will discuss the art of Christian civilization in order to demonstrate its ready acceptance of immobility and circular motion, especially in architecture, a branch of art which usually changed slowly since its foremost expressions lay in sacral and public political buildings.) Yet at a certain point there was a transformation from one worldview to another. Western people detached themselves from the cosmology characterized by immobility and from its traditional symbolization and aligned themselves with a new cosmology, the crucial juncture coming in the first centuries of our millennium. One of the little-observed but most important aspects of this new Christian cosmology was that it had no cosmogony to accompany it, that is, no myth about the birth of the gods.[9] It also had no theomachy, no story of the gods' internecine clashes, natural in polytheistic systems.

Genesis begins, abruptly, with a *monos theos* who creates the universe, the celestial bodies, animals, plants, and human beings. The first sentences remove all possibility of seeing in the stars any-

---

1979), 46-47. There is no question that the so-called primitive religious dances have a precise space in which the performers move, an unchanging rhythm, a song and significance. The dancers resacralize the ground around which they move, and they themselves are sacralized again, reinitiated. The exhaustion at the end of the dance (sometimes lasting days) is the way to commune with the tribal spirits, called forth by the tireless ceremony.

8. Ibid., 352.

9. While Christianity speaks of the birth of the incarnate God, it is a vastly different story from the births of gods—even the virgin births of gods—in other religions. The Christian version was surrounded by verifiable historical data, such as Herod's rule, the Roman census, and the governorship of Pilate.

thing but material objects. Two consequences follow: first, astral religion, common to all ancient people, becomes an impossibility; second, humanity alone bears the divine imprint and is capable of intelligence, independent judgment, and a grasp of the meaning of God's work. From the start of this monotheistic religion, humanity, not occult forces, gods, or daemons, was master of the world-all, and also a creator. The new teaching undercut myth, since the story of Jesus was contained in the Gospels and declared sacred and definitive. The later stories about Jesus which mythified his existence in the Gnostic lore and turned him mostly into a magician or an exalted phantasm were soon declared apocryphal and excluded from Scripture.

In sum, the presuppositions of a scientifically regarded universe were born, with no room for forces that might counteract God's creative and sustaining will. Nor, and this is most important, was there room for a cosmic model from which nations could derive their structure. The social order of Christian nations was, therefore, no longer regarded as a sacred order like the Indian caste system; instead it had freedom and autonomy, and the vast sphere reserved for historical and political action was now profane, essentially outside the bounds of religion.

The liquidation of the pre-Christian cosmos and the introduction of new cosmological postulates heralded a vast reorientation, first in astronomy and physics, then in the entire prevailing worldview. The foundation of the old worldview, which was still embedded in humanity, is well described by the Belgian philosopher Joseph Maréchal: "The human mind is a faculty in quest of . . . assimilation with Being . . . and it is perpetually chased from the movable, manifold and deficient towards the Absolute, the One, and the Infinite, that is toward Being pure and simple."[10] This view sees, then, an absolute point in the world-all (not in space but in spirit) in which Being is concentrated and toward which, as toward a gravitational ultimate, the multiple and the imperfect tend. This idea is clearly expressed in texts by Plotinus and Pseudo-Dionysius. For the soul this ultimate is God (for a time this was a common conception in Christian cosmology too), and

10. Quoted in Dawson, *Christianity and the New Age*, 40.

for physical objects this point is the place of rest toward which everything tends.[11]

The traditional universe is what Alexandre Koyré calls the "closed world," which he opposes to the "infinite universe." The latter was inscribed in the Christian worldview, however, and although it took centuries to make its impact on the philosopher and the scientist, when it finally did, the consequences for Christian cultures were incalculable. The infinite universe was not heterogeneous, teeming with life, and hierarchically organized. It was now emptied of multiple significances, interlocking mysteries and magic qualities (a process that Max Weber called "Entzauberung"), and rid of correspondences between high and low. When the abbots of Cluny designed their buildings with a view to capturing the world's meaning, they still acted in opposition to the new spirit which denied the fundamentals on which such a view rested. The new spirit, based on the new cosmology, carried in itself all the elements of the modern view of a uniform, homogenous space, where no one point was privileged, no one point was distinguishable from any other, except by an occasional local irregularity that further scientific observation and calculation could clarify.[12] In other words, in the Christian cosmology that is still ours today, there was no high and low, no tendency of bodies to seek their "natural" place, no causation in the processes of nature by psychic and supernatural forces.

The big change came about the time of the early Scholastic philosophers, who lived in the border zone between two worldviews and still accepted the Aristotelian physics which attributed qualities to bodies. In the cosmos of the Scholastics, writes Etienne Gilson, the movement of a body indicated the intrinsic mutability of that body, so the fact that a body ceased to be where it was testified to the possibility that it could also cease to exist.[13] Move-

11. Note, however, that the Gothic cathedral, as an object, completely contradicts this conception. While other objects sought their rest, the entire structure of the cathedral soared. The new "place of rest" was not earthly, it was God.

12. Jacques Merleau-Ponty, *Cosmologie du XXe siècle* (Paris: Gallimard, 1965), 43.

13. Gilson, *L'Esprit de la philosophie médiévale* (Paris: Vrin, 1944), 65.

ment was thus a quality of a body, one of many qualities, partly visible, partly occult. In contrast, writes Jan Marejko, the later mechanistic physics which took its guidelines from Christianity teaches that bodies "preserve their identity during movement."[14] The modern Christian universe is a homogeneous geometrical space where nothing has qualities—just as in the worldview of Democritus and Lucretius. There are no occult influences, no natural orientations, chosen directions, or astrological deductions; there are only mechanical forces acting according to laws established by calculation. This is not far from saying—and it *was* said in the seventeenth century—that God is essentially a master mechanic, a supreme watchmaker who had wound up the clock of the universe which then ticks off the centuries. This view leads to the conclusions of Deism, drawn a century later, that after having wound up the clock, God retired from creation and providence leaving the world clock to proceed on its own.

The new cosmology imposed the beginnings of a new self-image on late-medieval then Renaissance and post-Renaissance humanity. For a time, the hypothesis of a geometrically measurable, quantitatively perceived universe remained unacceptable to those steeped in the old geocentric tradition which seemed to be so much more "natural."[15] Although the "empty," geometrically describable heaven was implied in Christian doctrine, it found opponents within Christianity. The main reason can be traced to the Greek natural philosophers, first of all Aristotle, who taught the traditional proposition of a living, breathing, purposeful cosmos with its intentions and finalities. When Greek science was rejected,

14. Marejko, "Les conséquences philosophiques de la formulation du principe d'inertie," *Diogène* n. 123 (juillet-september 1983): 6.

15. I must call attention to the ambiguity of the terms *nature* and *natural,* particularly because the prevalent worldview of the past four or five centuries is again undergoing transformations through new astronomical discoveries and developments in the philosophy of science. These bring yet another astronomy in their wake. If the universe is again found to be a closed space, as some propose, and the creation theory is given new life with the assumption of successive explosions of an original hydrogen molecule, then what seemed to be "natural" from before the Renaissance until now will be relegated to the trash-heap of superstitions. However, no new cosmology has emerged yet.

some elements of the ancient tradition remained very strong and influential through at least the first Christian millenium, and some persisted well beyond it. This caused a conflict for the Scholastics that continued at least until Galileo's time. The Old Testament expressed a worldview, hardly contradicted by the New on this score, which was nearer to that of Aristotle than that of modernity. Yet at the same time, the demythified heaven of Christianity was *itself* the nucleus of classical physics and thus of the modern view. Even amid the elements of clash, the new cosmology was gradually coming closer, its acceptance less and less in question.

What were the consequences of this transformation to the new cosmological view? With the emergence of the theory supporting the homogeneous space and the infinite universe, motion could no longer be regarded as a transitory disturbance in the cosmos. It now acquired a new ontological status equal to that of rest. Indeed, in the modern view, according to the laws of inertia, a body has no tendency either to move or to rest; rather it tends in the absence of external influences to maintain its state, whether rest or uniform motion. The new cosmology also spelled the end of the view that bodies had inherent qualities. For mathematical and geometrical measurements it was meaningless to claim that bodies had such qualities as color, worth, beauty, or nobility. Humanity too became a machine, as thinkers from Descartes through La Mettrie to B. F. Skinner have maintained. Qualities came to be regarded as subjective impressions and emotional responses, different according to each of us. As Alexandre Koyré has noted, Galileo and Descartes declared that qualities are subjective in order the more credibly to present nature as homogeneous.[16]

* * *

Geometric space, the nonexistence of privileged points, the relativity of motion and rest, the nonreality of intrinsic qualities, objects and the universe itself reducible to mechanical laws—these were the bare bones of the new physical-astronomical worldview. It is a deanimated and desacralized view; it contradicts and op-

16. Koyré, *Etudes d' histoire de la pensée scientifique* (Paris: Gallimard, 1973), 190.

poses the character we recognized in the world permeated by the sacred. If nothing in the universe is privileged and nothing has qualities, then worship becomes a subjective exercise, suitable to provide a reassuring presence, however illusory, to those souls that need it. Worship then no longer requires public ritual, ceremony, decorative elements, or instruments of sacred mediation like the clergy or the sacraments. While the new scientific worldview had an uphill struggle imposing itself, it eventually was accepted, and Medieval, Renaissance, and baroque culture seem to have paid little attention either to what they had lost or to the philosophical consequences of the new view. The magnificent creations of these eras delighted the senses and the spirit with their architectural, pictorial, musical, and literary forms, yet they were paralleled by the severe, scientifically inspired worldview which implicitly denied their validity. These creations were a purely gratuitous play of the senses in the face of reality, which consisted only of colliding molecules. As Koyré observes, in an attempt to justify the new vision on other than pragmatic grounds, "Modernism replaced a qualitative and hierarchical cosmos by a universe, an open and indefinitely extending aggregate unified through the basic identity of the laws which govern it."[17]

Was it, however, a satisfying worldview on anything other than, possibly, scientific grounds? Koyré seems to hold that what nature lost in variety, it gained in the majesty of its laws, uniformly valid in both the heavens and on earth. This was the view of many seventeenth-century scholars and scientists. Their exuberance with the just-achieved insights into the workings of the cosmos gave them a quasi-religious sentiment vis-à-vis nature. Spinoza characteristically phrased it *Deus sive Natura*—"God or Nature"—by which he meant that *God* and *Nature* are merely two names for the same substance. Intellectual contentment, however, is no substitute in the long run for the awe with which the sacred was encountered in other cultures. A strange new situation began to arise.

In every civilization up to that point, the supernatural had been the repository of the realities that the society took for granted. The

17. Ibid., 197.

sacred that mediated the supernatural was intimately associated with the life of the society at every level of existence. While the sacred never became entirely a part of the human world, and while it was always perceived as different, yet it was experienced as operational in that world and was seen as the carrier of the supernatural. The new worldview overturned this conception. Its arrival was not a mere changeover from one sacred vision to another, as had often happened in the annals of humanity. The process was not like the conversion from the Canaanite idols of Baal to the Hebrew Yahweh, in which the displaced idols yielded, after centuries' struggle, to the other sacred, the one God. Nor was it like the replacement of the Aztec deities by Christ, which the contemporary Mexicans themselves perceived as the exchange of one sacred—spectacularly defeated before their eyes—for a new one.[18] It was much more.

The new worldview did not exhibit all its desacralized character by the late Middle Ages, or even for some time after. But by the seventeenth century it became an effective reality in philosophy (Spinoza), literature (Pierre Bayle, Fontenelle), and of course in science (Kepler, Pascal, and Newton). In the last, however, the rear-guard action was vigorous, because the scientists in particular remained unsure whether a divine substratum underlay the phenomena they observed. After all, they were as mysterious in their mechanistic clockwork precision as they had been for the traditional observer who saw in them vital forces in action.

Nonetheless, a new culture claiming absolute validity had unquestionably come into existence. Along with it was the growing awareness that the new laws, new political and social rules, and even scientific methods were not backed and guaranteed by the supernatural, and that therefore they were unreal. The added insight one gained into the how of a phenomenon was accompanied by no insight at all into the why. The result was a new cultural sensibility, evident in several signs. One was the sudden popularity

18. See Ursula Lamb, "Religious Conflicts in the Conquest of Mexico," *Journal of the History of Ideas* 17 (October 1956): 4. Lamb speaks of the Indians' amazement at the new and excessive freedom under the new sacred, and their disappointment that "no god tells them any more what is allowed and what is forbidden."

of works demonstrating methods of conducting inquiries, of adopting a set of behavior, or of educating (the ancestors of today's "how to" manuals). Another was the search for other substrata of phenomena, like alchemy and various other esoteric movements, some of which revived the Gnostic search for a god beyond God. A third was the westward expansion of various oriental teachings by the eighteenth century, encouraged by the developing spiritual void in the West.[19]

The dissolution of the supernatural guarantee on human affairs resulted in the need for new, human, guarantees. For several centuries, culture showed the various adaptations of this basic discovery: humanity creates for itself the meaning, the measure, and the law. It is unscientific and unmodern to search for them elsewhere, whether in the cosmos or in God's commandments and revelation. That there *is* no elsewhere was the message of generations won over by the varieties of humanism which added up to a syncretistic creed. It seems that from the decisive fourteenth to the twentieth century, still called "Christian centuries," the traditional worldview and the dominant forms of its sacred gave some support to Christianity, or at least collaborated with it. In many ways during this gestation period of modernity, the cosmic-divine model was still regarded as generally true, together with the channels which used to communicate its reality and meaning to traditional cultures. There was an intermingling of the pre-Christian, even the pagan, with the Christian worldview, producing a sensibility particular to four or five centuries. Not only did traditional practices

19. The search for an immanent and humanly manipulable "supernatural" is now also a characteristic of our age. In the last century, the search was suspended because thinkers thought they had found "natural" substitutes for the supernatural in science and in social utopias, both inspired to a large extent by Newton's towering achievements. Auguste Comte and Herbert Spencer, at the peak of humanist optimism, thought that they understood the "secret" of the social fact and that they had fashioned societal laws as scientifically as Newton had formulated his celestial laws. Since society alone was regarded as real, the problem of the supernatural could be considered as liquidated. It is, however, intriguing to observe that Comte literally "sacralized" Newton himself, who was to be adored in a special chapel—just as another "desacralizing" sociology, Marxism, later sacralized Lenin, lodging his embalmed body in a mausoleum.

and ways of thinking remain deeply embedded in rural populations (Eliade speaks of the Danubian peasants' pagan mindset), against which the clergy was to a certain degree powerless; but even more sophisticated classes up to the top of society were permeated, from marginally to completely, by the vision of a living cosmos— subsumed under the Christian God, most certainly, yet also having a parallel existence. It would be worth speculating on the extent to which these centuries were unconsciously transmitting the pre-Christian model of thinking and feeling, the tone of traditional life, thus partially filling Christian belief and practice with an alien, yet familiar content.

At some point, however, the traditional worldview reached its exhaustion. Not because Christianity finally triumphed over it but for a different reason: both the traditional view, suffused by ancient, pagan lore, and Christianity yielded to the scientific worldview. When and how? Georges de Lagarde needed five volumes to illustrate the triumph of the "secular spirit" in the fourteenth century; Paul Hazard fixed the date at 1715, the death of Louis XIV; Jakob Burckhardt, at the Renaissance; Oswald Spengler, at the migration of rural populations to the city. Lastly, Louis Dumont, without assigning dates or ascribing the change to events, speaks of the growing legitimation of the this-worldly, apparent in changing views of humanity. No longer were people seen foremost as *members*—of the cosmos and of a society still linked to the cosmos in which individuality received scant attention—now they were seen primarily as *individuals,* alone, with a completely mundane existence.[20] Dumont does not speak of the decollectivization of humanity, but he sees the Catholic church as an agent of mundanization.

A by-product of this phenomenon is that other areas of human existence, namely politics and the state, have emerged as carriers of universalist values. Ernst Cassirer spoke of the "myth of the State"; others have sacralized in their writings the secular state, the revolutionary state, or the welfare state. Hegel called the king a "hieroglyphic of power," and saw in the state the ultimate ex-

20. Dumont, *Essais sur l'individualisme* (Paris: Éditions du Seuil, 1983), 58.

pression of the collectivity as an organic totality and consciousness, a manifestation of the divine will.[21] Needless to say, this
sacramentalization of the state was an attempt of the secular spirit
to find new absolutes, since there was no longer any question of
finding in the state a replica of the cosmos or an agent of God's
will (St. Thomas called the state a "secondary cause" for God's
purposes with humanity in community). From the point of view
of sacralization this was obviously an impasse.

About the issue of individualized humanity and deified state,
many Christian apologists think along the line of Christopher
Dawson's statement that, at the very time that human beings were
at last acquiring control over their material environment (during
the four or five centuries of coexistence of the two cosmologies),
they were also abandoning the ideal of a spiritual order and leaving the new materialist forces to develop uncontrolled, without
any higher social direction.[22] This should come as no surprise—
there is a cause and effect sequence operating here. Christianity
called for mastery of the material world (did the church fathers not
call for the exploration of "numbers, weight, and measure" as a
necessary corollary of God's creativeness?), but that mastery was
bound to result in downplaying the spiritual. This was, after all,
the focus of scientific preoccupations throughout the very Christian seventeenth century, a turning point of Western civilization
between the spiritual and the material world. It was by no means
astonishing, however, as Dawson also suggests, that the latter was
chosen and the former deemphasized.

The issue in that century was whether arguments might be
found, to the greater glory of God, against skeptics and occul-
tists—against Pietro Pomponazzi, Giordano Bruno, Tommaso
Campanella, and Lucilio Vanini. God's rights had to be reasserted
in the eyes of the still largely Christian scholarly world, thus in an
appropriately philosophical and, better, scientific language. All his
life this was Father Marin Mersenne's ambition, and for this apol-
ogetic cause he brought together into a network of correspondents
men like Descartes, Gassendi, Hobbes, and many others. He

21. Hegel, *Grundlinien der Philosophie des Rechts,* par. 179.
22. Dawson, *Christianity and the New Age,* 95.

wanted it demonstrated that God moved the universe along pre-cisely functioning mechanical laws, that God's was a scientific mind. Mersenne may have succeeded too well. The Christian worldview did make its final peace with science, but the opponents were left unconvinced, drawing conclusions different from those expected or desired. If God is a superb mechanicist, then we can trust the automatic functioning of the world and our observations of the movements of matter. God deserved the few lines of intro-duction that Descartes gave him in his *Discourse on Method,* but it was matter, the *res extensa,* that henceforth absorbed people's attention. To sum it up, God was now an Epicurean. Lucretius, Epicurus's best-known disciple, began to be avidly read in the six-teenth century, although still only as a poet. Two centuries later Epicurean philosophy entered deeply into all modes of thought.

Yet the traditional view was not totally eliminated, even in scientific theories. One finds resistance to modern mechanicism in the writings and debates of Paracelsus, Kepler, Robert Fludd, Newton and many others. As the physicist Wolfgang Pauli writes, apropos of Kepler's theses, "scientific investigation is devoted to adjusting our knowledge to external objects; the archaic view should bring to light the archetypal images used in the creation of our scientific concepts."[23] The English occult scientist Robert Fludd answered Kepler's hypothesis thus: "Hermes Trismegistus says that the soul or the human mind (which he called the nature of god) can as little be separated or divided from god as a sunbeam from the sun."[24] The conclusion is that nature is God's emanation. The Nobel Prize winner Pauli sums it up in a way that casts light on the essence of the scientific endeavor, as much in conformity with traditional culture as with Suger's words. "For the Platonist, the life of the deity consists of a cosmic cycle which begins with the emanation from the godhead, first of souls, then of the cor-poreal world, and ends with the return of all things to God. . . . What is the meaning of this eternal cycle? Beauty, by virtue of

23. Pauli, "The Influence of Archetypal Ideas on the Scientific Theses of Kepler," in C. G. Jung and W. Pauli, *The Interpretation of Nature and the Psyche,* Bollingen Series, no. 55 (Princeton: Princeton University Press, 1955), 208-9.

24. Ibid., 215.

which all is drawn back again. The soul can do nothing but fit itself into the cosmic cycle in order to be a participant in the beauty
of the universe."[25]

Before Kepler, Paracelsus, an alchemist and physician, represented even more compactly the worldview here described. He
saw evidence for it in what he believed was a correlation between
humanity, the earth, the celestial bodies, and metals, as well as in
the permanent circulation of fire—a vital spirit of a sort— through
the cosmos. He saw God as the chief alchemist and saw astronomy
as teaching the relationship between human existence and the
world's reality. In all fields of knowledge—in a time when disci-
plines were not so clearly separated into "physical" and "spiritual"—there prevailed the idea of the organic unity of the universe and the multiple forms of emanation. C. P. Snow's complaint
in the 1960s about the bifurcation of "two cultures," the scientific
and the humanistic (a complaint that finds its place today in re-
ports about the "state of universities" and school curricula), would
not have made sense to Paracelsus and his contemporaries, nor to
the artists, architects, and philosophers whose imaginal and conceptual world had been shaped by premodern postulates. As
Charles Webster said in his Eddington Memorial Lectures in
November 1980, the pansophia of a Comenius was "based on the
ideal of the perfect integration of truths devised by reason or
derived from experiment, scriptural sources, and ancient tradition. . . . The continuing appeal of such ideas as divine plenitude,
metaphysical hierarchies, the existence of fundamental harmonies
and correspondences between the celestial and terrestrial world is
exercised through the intervention of a variety of spiritual agencies and intelligences."[26]

The view of the cosmos as a perfect, self-contained *place* was
complemented by the view of the self-contained nature of *time*,
since both space and time were creations of God. Both Paracelsus and Newton assumed that the planetary system is not eternal,
that it would come to an end in the near future. The imminence
of the "final age" was a deduction not from scientific data but

25. Ibid., 237.

26. Webster, *From Paracelsus to Newton: Magic and the Making of
Modern Science* (New York: Cambridge University Press, 1982), 10-11.

from the Bible, as was the imminence of the "last monarchy." Renaissance men like Marsilio Ficino, Pico della Mirandola, Agrippa von Nettesheim, and Paracelsus thought of themselves as possessors of magic means which could effect cosmic changes. Newton saw himself as a magician intervening between God and creation. His occultist speculations, related to alchemy on the one side and to God's design on the other, suggested to him that his own mechanistic laws might not be the last word on the structure of the universe. God cannot have initiated such impersonal and uniform celestial motions—namely, action at a distance—but rather must have ordained motions through contact, which would require a fine substance like cosmic ether. Newton supposed this substance to be a vivifying, celestial principle, an alchemical agent responsible for changes in the universe, an agent both vitalistic and universal in its actions, a "fermental virtue" or a "vegetable spirit," diffused through all things that exist in the world.[27]

In the seventeenth and eighteenth centuries, explanatory notions about the universe, motion, celestial mechanics, and attraction included the following: harmony in nature, parallelism between macrocosm and microcosm, pervasiveness of forces, animism, and emanations and hierarchies bridging the gulf between the material and the nonmaterial world. Even discounting the belief in beneficent and malignant daemons by some Renaissance thinkers, a belief rising from the occult tradition, it remains true that the Renaissance worldview presented a living cosmos traversed by impulses and intentions. The chief of these emanated from God, but there were also myriad others. Sir Thomas Browne, a physician, summed up his views of the mechanicist opponents of the traditional view on a notably alarmed tone. He asked why it was that "so many learned hands should so far forget their metaphysics, and destroy the ladder and scale of creatures as to question the existence of spirits. For my part, I have ever believed that

27. B. J. T. Dobbs, "Newton's Alchemy and His Theory of Matter," *Isis* 73 (December 1982): 514, 515, 526. The ancient conception of motion, still accepted in early Scholasticism, supposed that a body in motion was pushed at every terminus by the medium in which motion occurred. The body itself "would have preferred" to remain motionless.

there are witches. Those who deny it, also deny spirits. And are not infidels but atheists."[28]

Now the worldview offered in these speculations seems alien to our contemporary scientific, and also religious, discourse. In fact, it is nearer the ancient conception, although prestigious names of only two or three centuries ago, some of them revered ancestors of modern science, were among its adherents. This worldview, which one may call ancient, traditional, or religious, was the motor principle of various cultures, from immemorial times till yesterday. It formed the belief system on which culture rested and of which the creations of culture were taken to express evidence. Kepler's and Newton's image of the multi-layered physical-spiritual universe was not substantially different from that of Bach or Pascal, just as Dante's world was not very far from the three-story world of the *Iliad*.

It is important to note, especially for the discussion in the next chapters, that in this worldview the concept of power was always cloaked in the belief in a harmonious cosmos, with living manifestations at every level of existence. The cosmos was a "great chain of being," to borrow Arthur O. Lovejoy's phrase, and all knew their exact place in the eternal hierarchy. People took it for granted that a similarly modeled hierarchy also ruled the polity. While they accepted the worldly hierarchy with both resignation and admiration, they were at least reassured that this was the universal order, or the will of God, to which not only they but also the celestial bodies and lowly nature submitted.

*   *   *

We saw in previous chapters that in art too the traditional vision was reluctant to yield to the modern view. Desacralization dismantles the language of art, which was once foremost in mediating the sacred to the human. The numinous substratum fades from consciousness and from the unconscious, hence also from attitudes, so that the mediation is no longer a mediation of the sacred but only of its stylized version. Stylization means that artists and their art are detached from their mediational task. Artists begin to

28. Quoted in Webster, *From Paracelsus to Newton*, 89.

humanize and individualize their objects, and they then reduce them to miniature size and finally mass-produce them for everyday use, first by rich clients, then by the larger mass of consumers. The truly sacred object, however, the art of the traditional world, must be unique, an exemplary object. It may be reproduced only by symbolic contact, by reimmersion in the noumenon. It loses its numinous roots when communal worship yields to individual piety and taste. The members of the fourteenth-century bourgeoisie, Georges Duby writes, enriched with a relative suddenness, regarded the sacred objects they commanded for their exclusive use as objects of piety, to be sure, but also as vehicles of self-advertisement and ostentation, as status symbols. "Ornamental prayerbooks, jewels, small containers of relics . . . respond better than the vault of a nave to the taste of a society which liberates its aesthetic enjoyments from collective constraints."[29]

Total desacralization is reached when the former mediators—whether priests or painters—no longer perceive themselves in their original function but instead as self-contained ends. Emptied of the sacred—science is likely to take its place—the cosmos has nothing to communicate. People engage in the solitary creation of art so as to give meaning to the empty universe, but they can provide only personal meaning. When the mediators turn into individual sources of meaning, artists become a sacred caste and speak a language understandable only to themselves and a coterie of adepts. Furthermore, without an unambiguous language and mode of expression shared by the entire community, anybody can become an artist. Since there is no transcendence to communicate, artists shrug off the obligation to respect the real world which normally provides them with the elements of expression and no longer respect the laity with whom they ought to find communication. Lost is the true character of artistic style, which "is not the individual creation of genius, not the final result of a great number of efforts: it is the external manifestation of deep community."[30] Indeed, this is lost to the sacred in general.

29. Duby, *Le temps des cathédrales, l'art et la société 980–1420* (Paris: Gallimard, 1976), 240.
30. Vladimir Weidlé, *The Dilemma of the Arts* (London: SCM, 1948), 32.

Hans Sedlmayr, the Austrian art philosopher and historian, is a most illuminating guide on the subject of desacralized art. His juxtaposition of tradition and modernity is especially instructive because in his case a profoundly Catholic view is not divorced from a sympathy for pre-Christian modes of thinking. Sedlmayr observes that even Gothic and baroque architecture, both possessing an "airborne quality," recognize the "earth as their potential resting place to which they are related and to which they come soaring down."[31] In other words, the Aristotelian-Scholastic physics of "natural places" and tendencies for material objects was followed as the overall principle of sacred and profane architecture, from the pyramids to the baroque church, cutting through religions, civilizational standards, and artistic canons. Sedlmayr's stated preference for representational art is not just a matter of personal taste, it is also the discovery that even architecture has a story to tell, "picturing heaven or the cosmos." By telling a story art acknowledges its mediating function between the high and the low, the transcendent world (or cosmic model) and the human world.

Whoever would disbelieve the interdependence of a given cosmology and the traces that human beings under its influence leave in their environment—in politics, art, values, and conduct—has only to compare the artistic canons up to the seventeenth century with the canons bearing the imprint of the new sensitivity, beginning with the nineteenth. Sedlmayr discusses the phases of a transformation during this time. In architecture, there was a growing preference, quite obvious by the late eighteenth century, for spheres and cubes, mere geometrical bodies and outlines in buildings. On one level, these forms of the new architecture were simply objects of utility serving the needs of modern people, themselves now intrigued by machines and machinelike shapes. On another level, however, these figures implicitly waive all transcendental pretension and, inevitably, all organic relation to the earthly. A characteristic representative of the first level was the Swiss-French Le Corbusier with his mechanical apartment houses, incidentally unfit for human habitation, a mental abstraction carried out with a total impersonality in view. The second level finds il-

---

31. Sedlmayr, *Art in Crisis: The Lost Center* (London: Hollis and Carter, 1957), 98.

lustration in the skyline of most modern cities, in the cube-shaped office and apartment buildings (now also imitated by churches, schools, and museums), which readily give the impression of objects that lack an up and a down, that have interchangeable parts, and that strike the viewer as depersonalized and depersonalizing. We find that our cities, like the communities of the ancients, are exact replicas of our cosmology: but we have only an empty and homogeneous universe, inhabited by colliding molecules.

I need not emphasize that painting and sculpture follow architectural design in every age and culture, since the two are so often auxiliaries of buildings and interiors. Painting today is accordingly two-dimensional—not, writes Sedlmayr, in the spirit of Byzantine and Romanesque art in which the mosaics and paintings expressed otherworldliness, but as a way of suppressing the human element.[32] In contemporary sculpture there is an even more significant expression of the modern vision: the meaningless and formless, the tortured and the twisted material is a denial of the divine-human face and of the familiar localization of limbs, facial features, and proportions. It is as if through the negation of the cosmic reality, the reality of humanity were also expelled from our imagination; as if the spiritual craving were blocked with massive (Henry Moore), filiform (Alberto Giacometti), and floating (Alexander Calder) things, unable to introduce and identify themselves. Their solitary muteness is thrown in our seeking face as frozen signs of a dead universe.

*   *   *

The picture of the new civilization as it first coalesced, then gathered momentum, is revealed before us in all its clarity. I have proposed (though the thesis is fashionably contested) that cultures derive their content and contours from their cosmology, that communities form themselves in accordance with what they believe to be the transcendent reality of the cosmos. Those who disagree propose the reverse thesis: communities, they argue, project their mundane realities into the heavens as a cosmic replica, an archetype, in order to provide some sort of otherworldly justification. But this thesis unwittingly confirms what I just suggested: if so-

32. Ibid., 235.

cial and other mundane forms *are* in need of a cosmic or transcendental confirmation in order to acquire stability and credibility, then the cosmological picture is in fact first in order of importance.

This point requires no argument here. The essential discovery—not made on these pages, which merely elaborate on it—is that any culture and cultural epoch is dependent on a worldview, a cosmic reality. The traditional relationship between cosmic model and earthly replica was substantially modified by Christianity. Yet despite the rupture with the cosmic model that the Incarnation—the personalization of the God-humanity relationship—brought about, one cannot deny the continuity from the pre-Christian to the Christian worldview. In the latter's womb, however, there was growing the image of another, new cosmology that contradicted ancient physics and astronomy and desacralized the Christian worldview itself.

At the heart of this new view is its mechanical character, its silencing of the model world on which traditional peoples were dependent in their thoughts, beliefs, and endeavors. "The silence of infinite spaces terrifies me," wrote Pascal in the middle of the seventeenth century, speaking in that *pensée* directed to his unbeliever friends, the "libertines" (the name given to contemporary Pyrrhonists). Pascal himself was not frightened, both because he recognized God's creative presence in those infinite spaces—thus for him the spaces were not actually silent—and also because he trusted his intelligence and reason to fathom the universe. Yet if one lacked Pascal's faith, one would be thrown back on intellect alone to make sense of the world-all, now no longer a comforting, cosmic presence.

Between the new geometric-mechanical space and humanity armed with intelligence alone, there was now no longer a mediating sacred. As Nicholas of Cusa (also called Cusanus) said, the center of the universe is everywhere, the circumference nowhere. From where would the sacred emanate, and would humanity even need it as a polestar directing spiritual navigation?[33] A good il-

33. Nicholas (1401–1464) himself contributed to the desacralization of the traditional *and* the Christian worldviews by discrediting their character as a *picture*. Knowledge, he taught, can forever approach its object (including God) but can never attain it. The human spirit becomes more fertile the

lustration of the empty, neutral, geometric heaven is the cold starry sky of Immanuel Kant, who reads therein no comforting message. To moral law he ascribed no other source than himself; the ethical imperative is neighbor to, but no less dispensable than, the aesthetic impression created by contemplation of the stars.

What sort of people are these orphans of the desacralized heaven? The noticeable thing about them is that they are not aware of desacralization because they believe that the scientic worldview has satisfactory, in fact, advantageous, aspects. All inquiries suggest that most modern people partake in two equally blurred and low-intensity visions: they admire the scientific view as an ultimate answer to their questions, while a certain fluctuating percentage also believe that some nonhuman power is in command of "all that," particularly of their own fate.

This is a faithful reproduction of what modern cosmology suggests. Above is a desacralized, empty heaven, a universe in which objects collide or pass each other according to inexorable mechanical laws. Below rule the equally inexorable laws of earthly arrangements; here too people, interests, and ambitions collide and respond, according to psychological, sociological, and economic laws.

Thus to describe the vast realities of the new civilization in terms of the mechanical worldview is not difficult. On the individual level, people behave in the turbulent manner of gas molecules in a container; on the level of the mass, the intermingling turbulence of individual orbits creates a stable state, a dynamic equilibrium. The individual view, however, presents an incalculable anarchy leading to conflagrations, separations, and recombinations. On the scale of "social macrophysics," the homogeneous, geometrical space is reflected in political equality,

---

farther it sinks itself into the rational world that it creates in the process of explication. This process recognizes being itself as the "absolute presupposition," as the "most certain thing" in every question. "You, my God, who are infinity, can only be approached by him whose intellect is in ignorance, to wit, by him who knows himself to be ignorant of you." What remains is renunciation of knowing God and the search for a new method of exploring and understanding nature, waiting for the opportunity to dominate and transform it. Two Cusanus scholars, Ernst Cassirer and Maurice de Gandillac, see in him a bold originator of modern science.

since neither in heaven nor in the community are there privileged places and sacralized condensations. An egalitarian political structure is hard to imagine in a differentiated cosmos; and, inversely, the empty universe does not suggest to society an organization by orders and classes, with ascending privileges and conduct sanctioned by the hierarchy of distinct strata. It is noteworthy that the two leading political systems of the twentieth century, the democratic and the totalitarian, both claim endlessly to approach an "ideal equality," a regime of equal bodies (citizens) arranged in a geometrical-mechanical pattern.

*   *   *

At the beginning of this chapter I stated that members of any culture and religion have always asked three questions: How were the gods born? (forming a cosmology); Why did they fashion the world as they did? (forming an ontology); and What should follow in human culture (art, law, politics, science, etc.) from the divinely given structure? It is not clear that modern Western people still ask these questions. The inquiry may simply not make sense to them, or perhaps only the third question does. What we call culture remains the only point in focus; the other questions are meaningless in the modern worldview. Most modern people are convinced that culture is exclusively a product of human effort for which ultimate questions have no relevance; few realize that the question of culture cannot be answered without a prior and satisfactory concept of cosmology and ontology.

Our contemporary worldview is thus truncated and our culture remains a surface activity, almost a branch of sociology, based on the assumption that politics, art, law, and literature have no roots in a more fundamental spiritual reality. We are entitled to call it a desacralized view, one that has silenced the transcendent and blocked its channels. We should also point out that the crisis it has brought about is of the first magnitude: it has never happened before that a culture cut itself off from the deepest reality of being and advertised its autonomy. Because we are breaking new ground here, we are in a state of perplexity. We are facing, like Pascal's libertine contemporaries, the empty spaces from which we derive no meaning and no message.

Tolstoy's remarks in the epilogue to *War and Peace,* in which he speaks of historians who no longer understand the interaction of great men with the forces of history, are apposite here. For the ancients, he writes, such questions were answered by faith in the immediate participation of the deity in human affairs. For us moderns, who have rejected the faith of the ancients without putting any new conviction in its place, the question still remains: What forces move nations and civilizations?

In his analysis of power, asking what it is and why multitudes vest power in one person and submit to him, Tolstoy concluded that any definition would only prove circular: Power is the will of the power holder; it is the sum of circumstances for power to manifest itself; it is the need of human beings to be led. The peasant soldiers he described in his novel knew the answer—the sense of divine power in the affairs of humanity— better than modern people with their cosmic impiety. We may be less puzzled and less agnostic than the Russian writer. Whether under the cosmos or the personal God, power manifests itself as a reality, following from the structure of the universe. A force is implicit in the systematic motions of the celestial bodies; in the equally systematic functioning of citizens and groups of citizens around duties, interests, aspirations, and rights; and in permanently recurring events like wars, trade, worship, healing, and the education of the young. Only when no God or cosmic model is acknowledged, and all these things are attributed to chance or self-generated force (but what mechanism governs the "chance"; what "self" generates the force?), is power and the legitimacy of power also questioned. In the changing Western worldview, first came the denial of the cosmic model in the name of a personal God, then came the denial of the personal God in favor of blind mechanical forces, regarded as an adequate explanation for all observed phenomena, celestial and mundane. In the theory of political power this has led to the conclusion that politics consists of colliding bodies, the bigger ones crushing the smaller unless traffic lights are set up to avoid a collision or at least lessen its impact.

But then the next set of questions arises: Who gave the laws? Who shapes them as just? Who sets the limits? Who says they are to be obeyed? Can all this be done by mere reasoning, or does reasoning too point to a larger framework within which the ultimate reality of things is captured? The postmodern study of humanity, science, and politics, dissatisfied with the mere rational and hence with the empty universe, is attempting to provide new answers. While some may come tomorrow, today's universe is still silent.

CHAPTER FOUR

The Desacralization of Power

One is, I think, entitled to say that all political philosophies tackle one central question: What are the laws governing the eventual decline and degeneration to which all empires, kingdoms, and republics—indeed, all political structures—are subject? Along with this question is another: Can the downward course be arrested? that is, Can the political body be made stable?

For Plato, these questions were a life's work, and after him many other thinkers took up the same intellectual challenge. Some Christians sought in the Old Testament, especially the book of Daniel, a way of analyzing the rise and decline of empires in the past and from that some clues to what the future might bring. Some lay historians who thought they had discovered the universal laws of change were perhaps primarily interested in drawing from those laws the secrets of stability. Oswald Spengler's laws of inevitable decadence, which he saw as valid for all civilizations, in fact sought in a quasi-Hegelian world-spirit the answer to arresting decay. The fourteenth-century Arab historian Ibn Khaldoun, a "Spenglerian" before Spengler, saw in the recurring conflict between desert nomad and city dweller a means of locating laws beyond the nomad's conquest of the city. In more recent history, what was Mao Tse-tung's "cultural revolution" if not a way—as he himself admitted—of preventing the ossification and decay of the new communist empire under party rule?

Some of yesterday's political theorists say we should not discuss such concepts as decadence, change, and stability, calling

75

them "value judgments." Yet even if we replace the terms with more modern-sounding ones like democracy, orderly change, deconstruction, or the *Rechtsstaat,* the fact remains that there is still apparent in great civilizations a gradual transformation from the community's sacred structure and foundation under a divine order to a popular and individualistic structure. The transformation affects the political self-understanding of nations and governments. In ancient times, the change was from the authority of the temple to the power of the palace, a process observable not only in Mesopotamia, the *locus classicus* of scholarship, but also in Greece, where the process continued beyond monarchy to ever more popular and radical structures. The citadel that the king reserved for himself—and which may still be seen at Mycenae—moved down, as it were, to the public place, the agora, where the temple was no longer the expression of royal ideology but of the sacredness of popular power. In literature, too, we may follow the trend: from Homer and Hesiod, for whom the gods and a certain human fatalism dominate, we reach in less than three centuries Aeschylus, whose tragedies preach reconciliation between the savage powers of nature and instinct and the rule of law. Personal and family vengeance is rejected in favor of submission to the *nomoi,* the laws, the new divinities born of democracy and reason.

Some writers, including Jean-Pierre Vernant, the scholar of Hellenism, even suggest that the rational reorganization of the polis gave rise to philosophy. This is an interesting angle, characteristic of modern thinking, from which to view the origin of the state. According to this view, the state does not follow a superior model; on the contrary, it is a first datum, and its legal dimensions set the pattern for speculation in other orders. But in the case of Hellas, the legal dimensions themselves were products of the Sophists' philosophy, which was based, in turn, on a desacralized heaven and on a worldview later systematized by Democritus and Epicurus. Thus in a circuitous way we find ourselves back at our original contention: the political state reproduces the cosmological image of the community. But in proportion to its detachment from the sacred, and thus stabilizing, model, the state is launched on the course of decay.

A second observation underscores the remarks made at the

beginning of this chapter: civilizations have a general tendency toward desacralization, then decadence. What Vernant says about the Greek city-state others have repeated, mutatis mutandis, about the desacralization of the late medieval political community. The Christian ruler inherited his title from various converging traditions, Hebrew, Roman, and Christian. He was a *rex sacerdos,* a priest-king, and the states he ruled demonstrated the same course of the traditional relationship between temple and palace, a relationship well expressed in the term *christiana respublica.* At first, the interests of temple and palace coincided, since church and state represented two aspects of the unified and immutable cosmic-divine order perceived in Christ's revelation, even though Christians did not read their law in the cosmos but in the Incarnation. This law admitted no conflict-ridden pantheon, not even a heavenly hierarchy on the analogy of which king and pope could have argued about their respective claim to superiority. The pope's case was from the beginning the better one—not because the papacy antedated the empire (it did not) but because before God's tribunal it was the pope who had to account for the emperor's soul. The good order of the emperor's soul depended on how he had performed his tasks for the good of his subjects' souls; hence the pope had the duty to excommunicate a ruler who abused his position. Papal superiority over temporal rule was unarguably laid down in formulas from the time of Gelasius I (492–496) to Gregory VII (1073–1086). Together, church and state were God's creations; both justifiably ruled over humanity's spiritual and temporal welfare.

Needless to say, matters were not so simple in actuality. Temporal ambitions on both sides, escalating at times to armed clashes, modified the issues. The threat of excommunication gave the pope tremendous political leverage, since when the emperor's sinful state and deposition were proclaimed, his subjects, including rivals to the throne among the feudal lords, were no longer bound by their oaths and obligations, duties and loyalties. Theoretically, at least, when an emperor was excommunicated, he was outlawed, his authority voided, his person made a target.

Pontifical power would have prevailed in Christendom had not imperial and royal jurists, and later the humanists, challenged its absoluteness. They did so first in the name of the parallel sacrality of temporal rule, then in the name of natural law. They made a strong argument by reference to the Roman empire, whose laws were unanimously admired (did not Paul submit to them?) and which had no clergy independent of the law.[1] Imperial lawyers, and even some of the Schoolmen, argued that temporal rule carried in itself God's creative will, a fact manifest in the crowning of kings and the deference of popes and prelates. From Jean de Paris (1255–1306) to Cardinal Bellarmine some three hundred years later, many loyal members of the church asserted the limits of pontifical power vis-à-vis the temporal kingdom.

Thus the conflict and eventual separation between church and state (temple and palace) in medieval Christendom became an accomplished fact as it had in other civilizations. The relative moderation showed by the antagonists at the twilight of the Middle Ages was not due to a theoretical compromise but to circumstances. For more than a century the papacy was in serious difficulty, beginning with the "Babylonian captivity," the removal of the papacy to Avignon by Clement V in 1309, and ending with the Great Schism, the contention of papal power between pope and antipope from 1378 to 1417. Yet as the papacy lay prostrate, the partisans of natural law theories and the humanists began to criticize the foundations of secular power as well.

The late Scholastics, Otto Brunner writes, turned to the concept of natural law. Such a law, no longer bound to divine revelation but deducible from human reason, would be valid even if God did not exist.[2] The "conciliarists" used this conception to attack papal authority, but by the same token they undermined the emperor's authority also. Their position was that prelates and priests do not derive their spiritual efficacy through the pope but receive it directly, that is, from popular election and consent. This is how Walter Ullmann summarizes the situation: Rulership being no longer the affluence of grace, no longer considered as a divine

1. Walter Ullmann, *Principles of Government and Politics in the Middle Ages* (London: Methuen, 1961), 114. One could perhaps describe the late Roman clergy with a term used by Georges Dumézil: "technicians of the sacred."

2. Brunner, *Land und Herrschaft* (Vienna: n.p., 1943).

good deed, there was no room left for the mediatory role of the priests. There was, in the political field proper, nothing that could be transmitted, because it was already there. Government belonged to the natural community, the state. God as creator of nature had endowed it with its own laws, one of which concerned the establishment of the state and its government. All that before had demanded mediation was now clear, no longer needing mediation.[3]

This could be the epilogue to the centuries-long papal-imperial conflict; it was also the prologue to the (delayed) loss of authority and sacrality of temporal rule. It was quite natural that the first target of secularization (by means of the doctrine of natural law, as it happened) was the papacy, subsequently the state, and thereafter the very concept of power itself. Marsilius of Padua, one of the conciliarists, argued in his *Defensor Pacis* (The Defender of Peace) that two powers were one too many in a kingdom—or, for that matter, in Christendom. In view of defending peace, the people were to regard the pope as subject to councils, that is, to assembled Christendom, and thus merely as its executive arm. But since the emperor too should be authorized to call together a council and decide its agenda, the pope was to become a de facto imperial official. Henceforth it was not difficult, once the nonmediational popular principle was broached, to reduce imperial power too, shorn of its sacrality, to its democratic component.

At this point, let us find out what Thomas Aquinas had written on the matter in his attempt to locate an equilibrium between the contending powers. Taking for granted the permanence of the church and its spiritual and moral presence in society, Thomas emphasized the authority of the state as a divinely appointed agent of public order, a condition in turn of individual moral well-being and thus of individual salvation. On the issue of democracy he wrote that the political participation of a community's citizens was not a requisite of freedom, although, since neither God nor pope elects the ruler, it is understood that his authority is approved by the people for whose good it is established. Government for the common good is a practical everyday need; it has a reasonable guarantee in the observance of public peace. Thomas would have

3. Ullmann, *Principles of Government and Politics,* 260.

been less optimistic had he not been writing within the framework of the *christiana respublica,* in which spiritual authority was present to redress straying temporal rule. Medieval Christians took this for granted.

A generation after Thomas, Dante described the state as the rule of wisdom, penetrated by spirituality and preparing the City of God. Did he not place, next to Judas in the deepest pit of hell, the two Romans, Cassius and Brutus, for assassinating Caesar, the imperial symbol? In doing so he faithfully reflects the medieval notion of the sacredness of both church and state. Giles of Rome came closest to the traditional view when he wrote of the order reigning in the universe as the model to be approached by the government of the state. None of these men, however, could conceive the erosion of spiritual power and thus the purely natural character of the state that Marsilius of Padua taught, since up until then there had existed both the church as *corpus mysticum ecclesiae* and the state as *corpus mysticum patriae*. Between the two there had also been "infinite cross-relations," as Ernst Kantorowicz notes, mutual borrowings of prerogatives and symbols. The "*sacerdotium* had an imperial appearance and the *regnum* a clerical touch."

As we have seen, power in the West began losing its sacred character about the fourteenth century, the time of William of Ockham, Marsilius, and Jean de Paris. The beginning of this process was not evident at first, however, since the same period saw the rise of strong national monarchies whose claims were soon, at the Renaissance and after, to be supported by a still sacralized royal splendor, by the flowering of the arts and law, and by the newly formulated doctrines of absolutism. Pope Gregory VII's claim to authority in the eleventh century had been no more imperious than those of James I or Louis XIV in the seventeenth. The important point for our consideration is not how this process began but what its consequences have been. Thus we will pursue the progress of such ideas that Jean de Paris and others proposed already centuries before our time, namely that outside Christ there is no mediation in the area of religion and that reason is sufficient in the government of the state.

Many writers have described and explained the damage these blows inflicted on the view of the sacred as a condition and support of community. Some like Vernant suggest that the Middle Ages ended with the reactivation of the original, pagan *homo,* the unregenerated man of pre-Christian times. This is also the thesis of Ullmann, who then details the humanists' discovery that in the "ancient world society was ordered, governed and directed."[4] But it is not easy to see in pre-Christian man a "natural man," since the sacred permeated humanity's whole existence. On the other hand, Ullmann is right when he says that the "natural man of the Renaissance implied a de-sacralization or a re-humanization of the Pauline 'new creature.' Natural man, *homo animalis,* experienced a rebirth."[5] Ullmann describes a humanistic process to which he attributes political motives, just as Vernant saw in pre-Socratic, Sophistic "humanism" less a philosophy than a political project— in contemporary parlance, an ideology. Vernant alludes to the desacralized cosmology under Sophistic thought and writes:

> Instead of the ancient cosmogonies linked to royal rituals and myths of sovereignty, a new thinking was making way for a world order, based on the symmetry, equilibrium, and equality of the elements making up the cosmos. . . . Under the equality of laws for all [isonomy], the social world assumes a circular shape where every citizen is like any other. All describe the same career, occupying and yielding all the symmetrical posts which compose the civic space. . . . No portion of the world is privileged at the expense of another, no physical power is placed in a dominant position. . . . Supremacy belongs to a law of equilibrium and permanent reciprocity. In physical nature as well as in the *polis,* the regime of isonomy replaced monarchy.[6]

We cannot conclude here whether Ullmann and Vernant are correct in attributing to the humanists and the Sophists the state's turn toward secular ideals and, as both mention it, toward secular forms in architecture. We have indicated already that all the sacral paraphernalia of the later (seventeenth and eighteenth century) doctrine of absolute monarchy proclaimed as "divine right" were

4. Ullmann, *Medieval Foundations of Renaissance Humanism* (Ithaca: Cornell University Press, 1977), 10.

5. Ibid., 91-92.

6. Vernant, *Les origines de la pensée grecque* (Paris: Presses Universitaires de France, 1981), 7, 99, 121.

rather fragile vestiges of the earlier sacred substance manifest in the Middle Ages. Reading royal documents of the seventeenth century and examining the pomp surrounding the monarch (palaces, gardens, etiquette, costumes, pastimes, ceremonial occasions like dressing and undressing the *grande levée* at the French court), one has the impression of watching a baroque pageant whose flaming and exuberant forms are designed to hide the inner emptiness of and vanishing justification for a ceremonial shell.

Some of the more perspicacious observers, Pascal for certain, must have felt the incongruity between the royal display of power and the mechanistic science which was just then reducing the Christian cosmos to a neutral space. For a brief, idea-filled moment those in the scientific community, with imagination fired by the worlds now unveiled through the telescope and the microscope (Pascal's infinitely large and infinitely small), looked with awe at the rapidly succeeding discoveries.[7] Yet a few of them realized, with a new kind of terror, that there was nothing ontologically real beyond these lifeless and isolated objects. Beyond their orbits and vertiginous courses, better telescopes could detect yet more distant bodies, but this meant a mere enlargement of the viewed field, not anything meaningful for the human spirit. It now seemed only natural to apply reason and science to human affairs, with as much zeal as was dedicated to astronomical investigations.

$$* \quad * \quad *$$

The human affairs examined were primarily those of the body politic. The essence of power had to be reexamined since a great confusion had arisen as a result of the conflict between church and state, later between the absolute monarch and the rising middle classes and jurists, and finally between the Christian concept of community and the utopias proposed by humanists, savants, scientists, and *philosophes*. Democratic ideas had been proposed since the conciliarists of the fourteenth century, and Protestantism only strengthened them.

7. The French writer Fontenelle (1657–1757) describes how, one night on a terrace, he explained to a thrilled lady of the world the starry skies, harboring a "plurality of worlds." This became the fashion in elegant salons as Descartes began to be read, discussed, and popularized.

For several centuries after the Renaissance, thinkers were attempting to reconstruct the theoretically shattered state (the *christiana respublica* was long since a dead ideal) and, just as importantly, to justify the membership of citizens who increasingly stressed their individuality. A foundation had to be discovered for the two functions of law: enforcement of conduct by the authorities and development of links between fellow citizens. Up until this point, these had been taken for granted. The cosmic law and the divine law used to be unquestioned and were thus sure guarantees of empire, kingdom, and republic. For Thomas Aquinas and his contemporaries, whether philosophers or poets, law was the raison d'être of the state; natural law, ultimately unprovable but alive and valid, inspired the positive laws (the man-made laws organizing community life) that were derived from it by reason and prudence. Thomas insisted that law becomes law by being made public through the king's proclamation, a true authoritative act. The center of the law was its ability to coerce and punish, which presupposes the clarity and evidence of the natural and divine law.

That this presupposition had suffered in evidential power between Thomas in the thirteenth century and Francisco Suárez in the seventeenth may be ascertained by the latter's question: Is it possible for some to command others, binding them legally to obedience? His answer, however, was not different from that of Aristotle and Thomas. A polity built around the common good, he said, naturally demands subordination and civil obedience. Yet, with natural law itself in question, the notion of common good, hence of hierarchy and subordination, no longer commanded unanimity. Christendom was divided, and its fragments made contradictory claims on the place of the citizen, of the king's and magistrate's authority, and of the law. Significantly, the discord was increasingly based on the rising contribution of science, which was on the way to formulating the worldview in which scientific laws had greater plausibility than moral law in shaping the community.

These scientific laws were based on the molecular structure of matter and a spiritually mute astrophysics, that is, the earlier discussed conception of atomized individuals and an empty heaven. Faith and the cosmic image were no longer effective as cohesive forces of the community; the next to be proposed was a sort of political mechanics. We watch with fascination the rear-guard action as it took shape around the Galileo case. Cardinal Bellarmine and others argued that the physicist's propositions should not be rejected out of hand; rather, they should be granted the status of hypothesis until supported by further evidence. They pleaded that natural evidences ought not to be imprudently discarded. The Spanish Jesuit Benedict Pereira similarly wrote that in dealing with the "doctrine of Moses" we must be careful to avoid confidently saying anything which contradicts manifest experiences and the reasoning of natural philosophy or the other sciences. Since every truth is in harmony with all other truth, the truth of Holy Writ cannot be opposed to the solid reason and findings of human knowledge.[8]

The mechanistic worldview prevailed in philosophy and political thought. Thomas Hobbes, who helped form this new political vision, saw in human beings a mechanism without natural inclination for association, motivated by greed (*cupiditas*) and the fear of death and eventually entering upon a contract with similar human mechanisms.[9] Finally they submit to one elected official (the king), enforcer of the social contract. Yet his power, apparently absolute (Hobbes called the state "deus mortalis"), depended on the contract, that is, on his subjects' continued observation of it. They could indeed secede from the contract and initiate a new one elsewhere, with other partners. Jean-Jacques Rousseau, among others, made attempts to make the contract, once signed, binding. But this was a philosophical subterfuge: the signature alienated the signer's right to secede, because it was speculatively inconceivable that he would turn against his own will, now embedded in the general will.

Such circuitous reasoning, either by the more individualistic

8. James Brodrick, S.J., *Robert Bellarmine* (London: Burns & Oates, 1961), 352-53

9. The nature of these mechanisms or "atoms" is such that there is no correspondence between what they think or experience and external reality. "Pleasure, love, appetite, desire are but words to denote the same thing differently envisaged. . . . Concepts are nothing but motions impelled by a substance inside our head." Hobbes, *Of Human Nature*.

Hobbes or the more collectivistic Rousseau, remained unconvincing. There was the fact of rising democratic sentiments, but also the need to anchor the law, and thereby the state, in something more permanent than a temporary agreement. Marcel Prélot states the problem well: "Since democracy requires rules, and since such rules may not henceforth come from an external coercion, from a man who dictates his will, or from a social hierarchy with privileges, one can only derive them from individual consciousness."[10] Indeed. A contract is external to a person, and it dangles on the fragile thread of individual interests and their accord. On the other hand, laws and constitutions derived from a transcendent model were inacceptable to a humanistic age. Emil Brunner summed up the process in his Gifford lectures in 1947: first Christianity destroyed ancient religion and mythology; then modern idealistic humanism grew out of the Christian tradition; but humanism, following its rational tendency, finally detached itself from its Christian foundation.[11] There remained only the consultation of individual consciences, which were regarded, in the increasingly Protestant intellectual environment, as the most solid foundations of the immanent divine presence.

Law and government, no longer derived from an objective real transcendent model and no longer mediated by the ruler, become thus linked to the individual ethical consciousness, the only locus through which God speaks to humanity. This ethical consciousness was for Immanuel Kant the source of imperatives in practical, that is, moral, life. Laws are then rules humanity gives to itself, reassured by the immanent divine in the individual's self-awareness. It is evident that the law does not channel the sacred because the only remaining sacred is the human conscience—as Kant writes, it has built into it a normative instrument for free acts. The norms that I give to myself under the watchful eyes of my conscience are the foundations of the social sciences, in particular of legal science. Like causality among physical objects which is not to be found in nature but only in the ordering

10. Prélot, in the preface to Georges Vlachos, *La pensée politique de Kant* (Paris: Presses Universitaires de France, 1962), x.

11. Brunner, *Christianity and Civilization* (New York: Scribner's, 1948), 87.

mind, so moral and social duty is not located in the outside world (God's commandments) but is a mental category, that of practical reason. The external world is unknowable; its laws and modus operandi are inherent in the conscience. Because it is the subjective self whose categories impose rules on both physical and also moral phenomena, there is nothing to be trusted as real and as a source of judgment outside of what is written in the structure of the mind.

In discussions of the location, legitimacy, and exercise of power, Western cultures have lived by these postulates for the past two centuries. We have asserted that the final source of power is one's own conscience, assumed to be reasonable, decent, and in basic accord with the consciences of one's fellow citizens. Thus the vote and the entire electoral process are practically sacralized in our societies, and the citizen's will has, after "due process," the force of law, no matter how it may contradict moral law derived from other sources. We can see this in Kant, too, who saw those "other sources" as forever unknowable.[12]

The linkage between the theories of Hobbes and Kant (Kant obtained his own, improved Hobbesian view via David Hume) is obvious. The *contract* for the English thinker and the *norm-giving reason* for the German explain the political consensus predicated in our communities. We read in Kant's *Foundations of the Metaphysics of Morals* that "the principle of obligation is not to be sought in man's nature . . . but in the concept of pure reason alone."[13] Thus the validity of the law is not inscribed in a divine-to-human substratum; it follows from the Kantian category of obligation (*Sollen*), a sense of duty under reason's controlling eye.

Law for Kant, and therefore the whole concept of state and sovereignty, is relative. Law is no longer natural but subjective,

---

12. Plato, in his *Theaetetus,* attributes to the Sophist Protagoras the following discourse: "In politics as in justice . . . whatever a State believes and decrees is true for itself. . . . Even in the case of legislating for the future, the State is not bound by its own laws beyond the period that the citizens hold them as their opinion." *Theaetetus,* par. 176, conversation between Socrates and Theodore.

13. Kant, *Foundations of the Metaphysics of Morals* (Paris: Éditions Delahaye, 1971), 78.

and its contents now depend on time, circumstances, and majorities. This kind of gratuitous law eventually aquired some concrete validity—but how? The process was carried along in our century by the German legal philosopher Hans Kelsen, who adopted the Kantian postulate that we do not know the real world but know only phenomena. If reason's judgments operate only on phenomena, according to Kelsen, then laws are deducible from legal norms. Both fields stand under normative reason and both are mere conventions; but conventions are reliable sources of law since by definition reason never goes beyond them.[14]

This arbitrary presupposition has become the basis of contemporary political discourse. As Kelsen writes in his *Pure Theory of Law,* "Law gives itself the rules since legal procedure extends its norms as far as the fundamental norm; law in its application is creative of law." Just as in the Kantian view reason claims to establish the laws of nature, in Kelsen's thesis it is reason which establishes the norms of justice. The validity of positive law is independent of any norm found outside itself, in natural or divine law, for example. Even if one posits the existence of such immutable extrahuman laws, Kelsen argues, the rules of conduct ordered by positive law could not be obtained from them: from *Seins-regeln,* laws of being, ontology, one cannot deduce *Sollnormen,* moral obligations. Kelsen seeks to invalidate thereby the postulate of classical thought that being is intelligible and that the discoveries of intelligence are applicable to judgment and conduct. One has the impression of listening to Protagoras as one reads in Kelsen, "It is not important to know, for the validity of law, if its content, as established in the operations of positive law, is just or not. The norm of positive law is not a norm of justice. Positive law, in other words the set of constraints created by legislations and accepted conduct, is efficacious, and can never be in contradiction with its basic norm, but only with natural law."[15]

14. We may demonstrate Kant's and Kelsen's reasoning in this way: We cannot know reality. Because reasoning is locked up in the phenomenal world, only the phenomena are real. Thus only the rules imposed by the subjective self are valid since only they are accessible.

15. Kelsen, *Justice et droit naturel,* Annales de philosophie politique, vol. 3: *Le Droit naturel* (Paris: Presses Universitaires de France, 1959), 67.

The fragility of this line of thought—from Protagoras to Kelsen by way of Hobbes and Kant—is the more striking as these philosophers sought to provide the state with a solid political and juridical framework. Since the real and the good are inaccessible to knowledge, they say, what speculative system is capable of guaranteeing order and justice in the community? Such a system cannot be deduced from the (problematical) nature of reality but only from a rational system, itself based on a network of enlightened self-interest. Belief in such a frame of reference suffices to turn it into a habit, so that a "useful myth" arises, impressing itself on our mind as a second reality. Industrial-technological society has in any case constructed around us a world of conventions, rational and self-justifying, without a transcendent reference. We have thus become more receptive to other purely rational systems, juridical, moral, and political.

Kelsen himself points to the new nature of the state when he speaks of "the authoritarian state of ancient Greece which imposed its model on the cosmos, and promoted the belief that there is an analogy between nature and society."[16] According to him, the very idea of natural law is derived from the postulate of divine creation and of an ideal society in which superior norms function without impediments, inspiring the laws of human societies. These laws, Kelsen continues, would then be the norms with legitimacy in God's will. Such a conception assumes the existence of the "two societies" of the Platonic and Augustinian visions, an ideal society and a mundane, human one. But, Kelsen concludes, modern thinking has liquidated such a duality; it has emancipated the concept of causality fom nature's normative interpretation. The gain is that we need no longer search for a "natural law" above the positive legal order. From the scientific point of view (including the science of law), society is nothing but a part of nature, and there is no hypothetical order whose norms are applicable to society as we know it.

*   *   *

Motivated by the view that individuals behave in the manner of molecules in a container, or by the view (hardly a substantial

16. Kelsen, *Society and Nature: A Sociological Inquiry* (Chicago: University of Chicago Press, 1943), 233.

modification) that each carries a normative consciousness, modern
thinkers undermine the political sacred. The human political community has no transcendent affiliation, thus its place in the spiritual
world is abolished, its legitimacy subject to question. Even on the
level of the axiomatically held sovereignty of the people, Kant's
position was disturbing: "Electing its representatives, the people
alienates its rights. . . . Legitimacy abolishes the masses, and fuses
law and coercion within an indivisible sovereignty, embodied by
the holders of supreme power."[17] But if the voters cease being effectively sovereign the moment the vote is completed—as Kant
and Rousseau, two inspirers of modern regimes, hold—by what
right do the elected holders of power claim legitimacy? At least in
the traditional view the rulers did not have it in their ability to
annihilate the source of their power, the God of the cosmic order.

But there is more. The foundations of reason and reason's
norms are also undermined by the accelerating course away from
the traditional sacred. We modern people are told by psychologists, ideologues, and hermeneuts (also called "masters of suspi-
cion" by Nietzsche and his followers) that our conscious self is put
together from a mosaic of contradictory impulses, sordid interests,
secret desires, bundles of suppressed violence, and other tumultuous drives. Why should we then trust our "ethical consciousness"
which, even in the best of cases, is only one fragment of our ego?
True, Kant at the end of the eighteenth century saw reason as an
absolute sovereign, free of an intruding external world, master of
science and destiny. Yet his message about a proud reason with
sure judgments ill fits our newly discovered insignificance, our reduced status as an anonymous part of society's arbitrary and crushing structure.

Thus the fragmented modern worldview, so perplexingly different from the traditional and sacred one, has become directly
operative at the level of every citizen—the more so as the claim of
democracy and popular sovereignty intensifies the impression of
fragmentedness and involves multitudes in a confused quest for
some solid ground for the legitimacy of power and the state. The
political discourse, still permeated by the Kantian and Enlighten-

17. Kant, quoted from his *Rechtsphilosophie Reflexionen,* in Vlachos,
La pensée politique de Kant, 544.

ment optimism and confidence in reason, never touches upon the contradictions that the present century has come to imprint on people's minds and behavior. The few who try to emancipate themselves from the presuppositions of modernity make various efforts to bring into a new harmony such concepts as popular sovereignty, common good, legitimacy, and democratic representation. Their attempts suffer shipwreck because the prevailing cosmology in our culture—the empty universe of lifeless matter—cannot be challenged on the level of politics. The universe of political discourse reaches only as far as the ruling cosmology permits.

Nevertheless, the modern state with its democratic structure and welfarist inclination toward dirigisme brings all citizens under the purview of these issues. People have individual beliefs, senses of reality, and psychological predispositions; yet as citizens they are to accept the fiction of being tied to mere conventions, suspended, as it were, above the abyss of their own will. If nothing is real, if Hans Kelsen wipes God, heavens, and natural law from the screen of society's self-justification (or, as Hobbes would put it, from the screen of society's fear) as primitive notions projected by our obscurantist instincts, what remains as the foundation of community life? If power and the laws it erects absolutely lack the sacred in their origin and motivation, if legislators merely carry out the clauses of ever-changing contract, if law is but a "normativity" that reason gives to itself, then modern citizens find themselves weighed down by superimposed layers of arbitrariness. Their conclusion must neccessarily be that anarchy (molecular turbulence, in the physicist's parlance) is rational: I give the law to myself by means of my own sovereignty yet I find I must bear the burden of a huge bureaucratic apparatus that is unable to justify itself. Well then, why not discard it? Why not bypass the entire bureaucratic machinery—which in any case claims to register and execute my own will—and give the law directly to myself?[18]

18. We saw above that Rousseau, who grasped the logic of this reasoning, attempted to respond by recourse to the "general will." He forbids citizens to hold this kind of anachistic discourse because once they deposit their freedom to decide on the altar of the general will, they become encrusted in it and lose the right to criticise the magistrates, the executors of the social contract.

Whether citizens actually hold such a discourse or not, it is an anarchistic thesis because in their perplexity they do not apply it only to the modern bureaucratic state but also to manifestations of power in general, to the state as such. The latter has ceased to exist in its traditional form, with roots in a transcendent reality, yet the new state without foundation claims autonomy, self-sufficiency, and the mutual transparence of its citizens in their dealings with the state and with each other. All claim to have driven out their daemons.

With the exclusion of the daemons, however, the sacred also departed. And now this radical demythologization places, in turn, a staggering weight on the "social question," a weight perhaps equal to that of the discarded sacred. In their endless procession, the problems of the collectivity become the new daemons obsessing the citizens. The presence of the sacred used to provide the community with a sense of proportion which relativized social phenomena against a common and legitimate standard. The political and ideological garb which now attires every so-called problem signals its elevation to the rank of an idol. Everything has become crushing and urgent, everything demands equal and immediate attention. What is important enough now to deny or delay the citizens' rush for instant satisfaction?

CHAPTER FIVE

Power in a Desacralized Milieu

The last chapter's closing question about the "instant satisfaction" of citizens may seem to point at an ideal commonwealth with members living according to the rules of strict equality, all of them democratically participating, all of them happy. This ideal picture is, of course, unreal. No human community is "happy," nor do all citizens participate equally. The vocation of the state is not the happiness and personal well-being (*eudaimonia*) that Aristotle reserved for the well-balanced man of contemplative virtues; nor does the state seek as its goal the satisfaction of all competing and tumultuous interests. Rather the traditional state sought the best way to effect the principle of unity and order. Yet our civilization has cast aside even this principle, which is clearly present in the traditional concept of a transcendent and divinely willed model. In truth, the modern state is based on the denial of such a model and therefore on its fragmentation along the lines of another principle: the primacy of the individual.

. The modern political objective is to set up a collectivity which functions like a self-regulating machine, like a mechanical universe with self-given laws of motion. The main purpose of the state is the satisfaction of individuals, a policy which does not take into account the price that the community as a whole must pay for such a mechanical juxtaposition of competing interests and the resulting conflicts. The price is high. High because "individual satisfaction" is measured in mechanistic terms best formulated by John Stuart Mill, who stated that a citizen's movements (freedom) have but one limit, the identical but perhaps contrary movements of other citizens. High also because such a law, so evidently derived from what our contemporaries read in the prevailing cosmic image of mechanical motion and collision, leaves out of its calculus the common good which implies the observance of a scale of values by the governing agencies.[1]

In sum, individualism presides today as the legislating principle and the exclusive philosophical justification of political and social thought. This is an Enlightenment view, easy to compress in a few words of Diderot: The individual is the only existent; he needs society as a temporarily paralyzed patient needs crutches. At the end of convalescence, he will throw away the crutches. All modern utopias, from Renaissance tales to liberalism and Marxism, are based on this premise: Whatever constricting laws and rules now imposed merely serve the final objective, humanity's return to unaided individuality and freedom from social constraints. Modern societies and political bodies are thus locked between the formulas of Diderot and Mill.

Not only are these promises of utopia not kept, they are groundless promises because human beings are *animales sociales* for whom society is neither a nuisance (J. S. Mill) nor a temporary crutch (Diderot) but, on the contrary, the means of becoming truly human. Living in society is a positive good, a qualitative leap over mere individuality. In short, society too has rights built around the presence of the sacred, as we have seen all along in our examination of the traditional concept. Today's loss of the sacred thus becomes intelligible in political terms when we diagnose it as the fragmentation of the common good into individual rights, interests, and preferences. The latter are set down as meticulously formulated laws which not only take precedence over the social

1. Both dominant political traditions in America, individualism and pluralism, one derived from Madison, the other from Hamilton, identify happiness with property and material pleasure, according to John P. Diggins in his study of the foundations of liberalism. He adds that neither tradition committed America to political ideals that appealed to one's higher nature. Individualism provided the means by which Americans could pursue their interests, pluralism the means by which they could protect them. See Diggins, *The Lost Soul of American Politics* (New York: Basic, 1985).

nexus but in effect destroy this associative tissue of the community.

In societies in which the transcendent model has a directive role the social nexus regulates a substantial part of one's conduct towards others, not because the community is necessarily small but because its members know and recognize their own and everybody else's place under the model. In the main axis of social identity is the power relationship between ruler and citizen, which sets the pattern for the entire social fabric. Through his participation in both levels of reality the ruler was a mediator and transmitter of beneficent emanations of the transcendent to the mundane community. True order, in the formula of Pseudo-Dionysius the Areopagite, is the dependence of the lower on the higher. Without such a fixed and transcendent order, writes W. Kirk Kilpatrick, everything becomes arbitrary; thus we have instituted the rule of law to provide the fixity we need. As a community's belief in the heavenly standard to which to compare its behavior wanes, it becomes ever more dependent on law. In such a society—ours is a good example—law has to work overtime. Soon, however, the purely legal attempts to provide and maintain order are bound to fail since law itself is eventually revealed as arbitrary. Cut off from its relationship to the supernatural order, the law cannot bear close examination. Much of the moral confusion in our society, and much of the weakening of traditional modes of authority, stems from the extension of contractual order into areas which were once the realm of the sacred and natural order.[2]

The process of the desacralization of politics is the change from alterity—the essential otherness of the cosmos over against its mundane replica—to identity. The alterity of the cosmic-divine model requires the sacred as a mediational channel. But as the

2. Kilpatrick, "Why the Secular Needs the Sacred," *Human Life Review*, Winter 1984. Under excessive legalism, material satisfaction reaches grotesque proportions. Many people today argue that a fetus's right to life does not entitle it to use a woman's body against her will. To give a specific example, Carole Tongue, a British Labor member of the European Parliament in Strasbourg, requested investigation of the Vatican's refusal to ordain women as priests. This refusal, she argued, is incompatible with Common Market regulations for equal employment rights.

function of rule becomes socially articulated and more agencies arise within the scope of power, these agencies acquire a modicum of independence as bureaucracies, and power is increasingly shared. Alterity gradually yields to identity, power is stabilized at the lower level and passes into the hands of individuals and popular assemblies. As Marcel Gauchet sees it, the king, vicar of God (or transmitter of cosmic forces), transfers his power to lower strata, prompted by his repeated clashes with challengers.

In pre-Christian political configurations this transfer and broadening of power was largely avoided because the temporal was never granted an existence independent of the spiritual and the cosmos acted with a monolithic force. In Judaism, the prophets effected a split in the monolith in the name of Yahweh, who was angry at the kings and the nation who strayed from his path. In Christianity, Christ "officialized" the cleavage by legitimizing both the spiritual and the temporal through the Incarnation. In the interstices opened in the *christiana respublica* by the ensuing conflict between church and state, both sought allies to whom concessions were then granted. We saw in Chapter Four that the state finally won the contest, but only by diluting its own power: it consented to a vast desacralization first of religion then, in turn, of politics. Henceforth, regimes based on the principles of individualism excluded from their purview the sacred and its mediation; their only source of legitimacy has been the law that they give to themselves through the fiction of popular will. The words of Georges Vlachos quoted in the last chapter sum up the present situation: the rules of democracy cannot come from external coercion nor from a recognized social hierarchy; they must come from the individual consciousness, since a thorough secularization permits no transcendent or even moral reference. The origin of law must be sought in the arbitrary and the conventional (Hans Kelsen); it must come to rest in the majority.

While political authority appears more independent today than ever, it actually submits to a permanent revolution of the mundane order, in proportion as it is deprived of its symbolic base and sacral identification. Mediation, the traditional prerogative of authority, has been taken over by the (Kantian) individual conscience, now the sole entity allowed to maintain a relationship with God, though it must always remain a strictly private relationship.[3] No institution mediates any longer, and the state itself claims to be nothing more than the neutral crossroads of plural interests, all of them mundane.[4]

This view of power as the sum of individual interests leads to the sacralization of the individual, cogently expressed in the term *human rights*. Clearly God no longer has any rights except that of private conversations with his worshipers. "Human rights" now goes beyond the citizen's right to be protected under the law against crime or unsafe conditions of life and work. It means the annexation by the individual of what used to belong to the spiritual and political spheres. Ultimately it means the final and exclusive legitimation of the this-worldly order. Human rights are not derived from a higher source, they are not the rights of the person as a child of God. Rather they follow from one's individual autonomy (described as "intrinsic dignity"), from one's own internal leveling and mechanization, as a result of which the right to the "freedom of sexual expression," for example, is seen as equivalent to the right to be protected against enslavement or assassination.

Endowed with the plenitude of sovereignty, modern individual citizens choose from a wide variety of options in their attitudes and actions in religion, lifestyle, sexuality, morality, education, cultural orientation, and use of leisure time. Such choices were always available to the superior man of the past, but there are now two novelties: the availability of choice to everyone creates the impression of uniqueness and superiority for all; and the fragmentation of religion, politics, and culture no longer requires the individual to overcome the resistance of institutions, norms, and standards of excellence. Everybody possesses not only human

3. Note the prohibition of public prayer in public schools.
4. We may occasionally observe the state's embarrassment in the realm of religion—for example, when it had to decide several years ago whether the Rev. Jim Jones's sect, which later committed mass suicide in the forests of Guyana, was a "religion" or not. Having no standard by which to judge, and acknowledging no competent spiritual authority whose judgment it would accept, the state and the courts were obliged to decide that Jones's sect was in fact a religious community and should be granted all the secular privileges attached to such a status, like tax exemption. Another example is the state's view of satanist cults.

rights but also diplomas, certifications of talents, artistic abilities, religious insights, and personal ideologies. Everybody is an "individual"—it is no longer a merited title. All values are equivalent since everybody has one or more, and choice among them, with subsequent choices and "commitments," is regarded as the right of the consumer to consume. As a consequence, individualism has quite logically degenerated into "massism" and uniformity, thence into a battle of minor gods whose clashes are the more ferocious as none can excel for lack of real standards of achievement.

It may be worthwhile briefly to examine two great men who truly deserve the label individualist and to see how their individuality fit their age and how it shaped two different senses of individuality. The first, Dante, represents the traditional sense; the second, Goethe, the modern sense.

The difference between the two lies not primarily in the centuries which separate them but in the manner in which each conceived his creative relationship to the cosmos. Dante, no less critical a mind than Goethe, submitted to the worldview of a harmonious plurality. He had no difficulty in situating himself between heaven and hell, in the world of sin and redemption, within historical time yet in preoccupation with the eternal. Angels, sinners, murderers, and saints; the procession of history and salvation-history; the advance of science and representation; the mundane concerns of politics, papacy, emperor, and the Italian cities— all were his home ground. A great artist, he did not choose new forms but filled the existing ones with a new content. As Titus Burckhardt observes, great artistic geniuses bring out new values, neglected or unknown until their time; but they also work within a spiritual economy which limits their themes and their methods. Thus Dante became an architect with words, a musician with rhythms, a magician with images. He shaped his times and was shaped by them, a teacher as Homer had been for the Hellenic and Roman world.

Yet when we think of Dante we do not have an "individual" in mind in the modern sense of someone seeking (and tormenting himself in the process) originality of topic and style, shock-effect, a demiurgos-like inventiveness, adding the disfigurement of self to the artistic personality. Our attention while reading Dante is not drawn to his person, just as we are not especially attracted to the owner of the modest signs or initials that occasionally remained on a medieval painting, statue, or carving. The importance of such a sign is absorbed by the artwork to which it belongs. Dante the individual takes second place behind the poetic monument and its central hero, the divine being.

Goethe on the other hand is the paradigmatic individual in the modern sense, searching for his way all his life. His contemporaries and biographers describe him as a "genius," a term that to Dante would have seemed usurped. Nothing was more natural for Goethe than to choose subjects from his own life: loves, sufferings, travels, triumphs—the *I* is always present under the borrowed fictional disguise. His confessed intention was to construct his personality, thus to choose and reject the unoriginal as useless. He looks at himself from outside, becomes his own double, follows one pattern then another, always aware that the double, triple, multiple character adds to his stature. He is the jocular rhymer, the forbidding court official, the flatterer of the great, the self-analyzing lover, the burgeoning or mature genius. It cost him a great deal to keep all these threads in a supreme, organizing hand, and he allowed them to loosen only when his two central occupations overtook him: poetry and science. While Dante in the *Divine Comedy* glorified God's creation in which he made a place for himself, Goethe *is* his *Faust*, a new creator. While Dante fit effortlessly into the sacred that he found at birth and wove further embellishing threads into its fabric, Goethe put his art in the service of the new sacred: individual destiny.

This detour into literature helps to clarify the conflict of individualism and tradition by means of two prototypical figures. At the same time, it also points at a difference which does not carry a judgment of values but implies two ways of being, two modes of envisaging the world and one's self in it. Not everybody is Goethe, not everybody can draw together centrifugal trends as he could toward the end of his life. The fragmentation of modern individualism is such that it rarely produces a great individual capable of overcoming the pull of divergent and discordant forces and harmonizing opposing tensions. The usual consequence of individualism is that one follows one's own law, urged on not by the fervor of the Goethean search for unity and uniqueness but by the anomie of modern living. A further fragmentation occurs when this day's monoliths of conformism yield abruptly to tomorrows's monoliths, with the effect that the slogans and behaviors of yesterday are no longer even recognized under the pressure of new clichés and conducts. Thus we witness a fragmentation of time as well, which leads to resounding yet monotonous controversies between groups of citizens using different codes, different languages.

Controversy thus becomes the element most familiar to the modern individual, our natural milieu. Conflict is unavoidable and necessary—and also endless, because while one is supposed to feed the controversy as an essential part of one's civic right, the rule is that nobody is supposed to or is expected to win by argument or by naked force. It is evident that we are not far from that other mark of modernity, the Marxist class struggle, also never expected to end, also a way of stamping the social fabric with characteristic conflict. The "end of the class struggle" is a millenarian ideal whose force resides precisely in its unrealizable nature. In the meantime, a whole social organization comes into being in its name, serving as an unprobing proponent of political thought and action. The "end of the class struggle" or the "total democratization of society" becomes sacralized, the final justification and the pole of orientation.

We have just described the unavoidable and necessary conflict in modern society in its liberal Western version. Just as "class struggle" in Marxist societies is not really supposed to be won by either class—while the myth feeds itself on Manichaean presuppositions and collective passions—because then the regime's raison d'être would collapse, so the conflict in liberal societies must not be won by any party either.[5] While the conflict lasts, it pro-

5. George Orwell imaginatively captured this aspect of modernity in his book *1984,* in which three identically totalitarian world empires are locked in an endless series of wars, two against the third, then in another permutation. There are no genuine issues or clear objectives to be won. Orwell must have understood that the heart of modernity—systematized by Hegel, Darwin, and Marx—is conflict and violence. This is also implicit in Schopenhauer's and Nietzsche's concept of the will as the substratum of an otherwise unfathomable existence.

vides great benefits. Alexis de Tocqueville remarked about American society that its principle of cohesion is not virtue or the striving for it but the play of material interests which imposes a certain discipline on all members. This is akin to Adam Smith's insight a century before into the nature of liberal societies: provided it is allowed free space, the conflict of interests, talents, opportunities, and ambitions leads to an overall harmony. Virtue consists in following a self-chosen course, trusting that in acting in one's self-interest the apparent irreconcilables will, in due time and at a given level, be harmonized by some "invisible hand." (It is not difficult to find here the impact of modern cosmology: the rushing bodies impelled by blind forces constitute the universal harmony according to mechanical laws of which the bodies themselves are unaware.)

When Irving Kristol describes America as a "bourgeois civilization," a "commercial society," a "prosaic [desacralized?] society" living under "liberal capitalism," he sees at the nation's roots the same thing that Tocqueville saw, that is, self-interest.[6] Kristol acknowledges that individual interest in American society is the principle of differentiation—over against societies rigidly divided into classes or castes elsewhere. He does not pursue the matter as far as Marcel Gauchet, though, who insists that the main social code and requisite of modern society is that nobody is allowed to win, that nobody may be right. Conflict is then the essence of freedom, the red badge of individuality, really a kind of common good in reverse. More than that, conflict has the vocation of being turned into a religion. Andrew Greeley and Jeremy Rifkin have concluded that John Stuart Mill's postulate, "my freedom of action stops at my neighbor's freedom of action," has a behavior-dictating power that only religions have; religions call it morality and assign to it other limits and other ends.

In the society here described, whose exemplar is the United States, there is no arbiter, for none would be allowed to function. All citizens and groups are ideally equal parts of the mechanism, and whatever temptation there exists to rise above the rest and ex-

---

6. Kristol, *Reflections of a Neoconservative, Looking Back, Looking Ahead* (New York: Basic, 1983).

ercise authority outside the constitutional limits is deflected toward the accumulation of material goods as the chief and authorized form of satisfaction.[7] But even the wealthy acquire their fortune with the tacit toleration of their fellow citizens. They are seen as exemplifying the desires of—with the approval and will of—the others. Thus the power of the wealthy in the American myth does not lead them to political results of any magnitude. Leadership may not even be in their consciousness as a clear perspective and ambition.

Not the smallest paradox of "individualistic" societies of the modern American sort is that the role of the exceptional individual, a locus of potential power, is severely restricted.[8] Indeed, if every aspiration outside a few well-controlled and quasi-prescribed channels—law, business, and politics—is privatized, as are religion and culture, then the individual is brought down to the level of routine thinking and action. Santayana noted the paucity of channels in which brilliant members of the individualistic society can direct their talents and energy. They are tacitly obliged to work within the favorably regarded activities (note the three above) so as to remain in the public eye; the collectivity dares not allow them to open new roads (and prevents them from doing so by removing the prestige from sheer ambition), for they may carry themselves to new positions of power. The restriction and channeling of individual ambition are meant to limit the conflict inherent in society to individuals (who compete, for example, for success in business, sports, politics, or litigation), and to certain carefully controlled institutions.

Modernity, in both its Marxist and liberal forms, selected religion not unexpectedly as the first target for privatization, which virtually grants religion outlaw status, considering the communitarian dynamics that it possesses. Religions institutions were

7. One could say that the genius of America consists in the reorientation of talents toward channels of material success.

8. The common usage of the term *leadership* often occults the real meaning of the word. It has become a platitude: an ability to direct majorettes, collect funds, or become popular. It does not often mean the direction of an original mind and strong will, which sets ideals and mobilizes people to carry out bold projects.

privatized because from them may come a formulation of the common good not based on conflict and competition. They have also been the immemorial source of transcendence, thus of an order other than the worldly social arrangement, and they have been the channels of the sacralization of political power. Through the privatization of churches and of the religious discourse, an additional objective was also reached: the political neutralization of those talented citizens who, with the passion of transcendence in them, might enter the religious vocation and refashion the social landscape on other than an immanentist pattern. If the church is privatized, so is the soul filled with faith.

In Marxist societies, which often actualize what for liberal societies are only latent projects, the process of religion's privatization and quasi exclusion is abrupt and brutal. Within a few years of taking power, Marxist regimes make it clear to people of the church that they will be at best tolerated in a well-defined and assigned corner of the new society until the moment of religion's final liquidation. The liquidators are named and appointed and organized as the Bureau of Cults, an agency of the ruling party. In Budapest in 1985 the Bureau defined the permissible sphere of church activity as follows: the churches "fulfill a positive function insofar as they strengthen socialist [i.e., Marxist] unity, spread the humanistic ideals, exhort workers to produce more, combat criminality, preserve historical monuments and encourage scholarship, participate in environmentalist activity, and in other fields."[9] Such activities may be the task of government agencies—or of private agencies in a liberal society—but they have little to do with the religious mission, faith, and the moral influence churches possess. The program is thus a warning that certain limits should not be overstepped, in exchange for which the regime grudgingly allows some regular but supervised contact between private individuals and their faith. Both the church and the believer are kept under the Bureau's watchful eyes so that the practice of religion takes place, as it were, in a locked area, in the quintessential private.

In the real area of everyday occurrences things may be less

9. From an interview with Imre Miklós, chief of Hungary's Bureau of Cults, in *Magyar Hirek,* Summer 1985.

constricted. They may resemble the situation in liberal societies which apply their basic Millian principle—your freedom stops when it encroaches upon mine—to churches with a hypocrisy greater than that of the Marxist regime. Indeed, the principle encroaches on the church's proselytism—not in the sense of supervising individual intentions and practice but in the sense of curtailing the means by which proselytizing may be carried out. Religions breathe through public symbols and expansion in the public space. Being restricted to a private status, on the other hand, not only limits religion's spiritual effectiveness, it also reduces it to equality with other institutions. What used to be a vocation at the center of society, the channel manifesting spirit and power, becomes a legal and social equivalent of cultural institutions—of hospitals, museums, and schools. It becomes merely one of those agencies which care for our general well-being. When religion becomes pluralized, writes sociologist Peter Berger, it is obliged to submit to the law of competition. It must make itself credible and desired, since it is no longer able to impose itself by its own authority. It must be sold to a clientele no longer compelled to buy it. Religious institutions turn into agencies of market organization, and religious traditions become consumer goods.[10]

When liberal society restricts religion to the same marginal function that Marxist society does, the difference is only that the former uses no threat of physical extinction. In reality, however, it reduces religion to irrelevance as effectively as the latter. In fact, perhaps to an even greater irrelevance, because the religious soul in Marxist regimes, under the pressure of the governmental apparatus, learns how to resist direct oppression and coercion and reaches out naturally to the church as an unofficial hierarchy parallel to the state. In liberal societies where there are no powerful secular hierarchies comparable to the Communist Party, and where institutions hardly rise above the flat landscape, the soul either finds no support or finds various social gospels preached under every roof.

10. I think here of a publicity campaign directed by the Archdiocese of New York during Christmas 1985 for turning or returning to the Catholic faith. One sees in a television commercial Mr. Average Man pass by St. Patrick's Cathedral and then decide to enter.

Another consequence of the neutralization of religion in liberal society is that the offer of freedom to all and in equal measure lures churches into the false belief that their vocation is to accept the liberal postulates and pattern themselves on loose liberal institutions.[11] The temptation comes in many guises, one of which is the freedom to advertise, to make money, to own property, and to be a welcome guest of the media. The combined weight of these spectacular "breakthroughs" to the avenues of publicity from the shadow of the secular power in which the churches had lived since the Enlightenment is such that the social penetration of Christianity in liberal societies is now measured by statistical data. Greeley and Rifkin evaluate the spread and depth of religion in America—its "success," in other words—by such phenomena as multimillion-dollar television programs and other business activities in which the churches engage: fundraising, advertisement, building projects, and so on. When churches put on a worldly garb, they naturally lose their specific features and vocation. Catholic schools in France and the United States have adapted themselves to the public system, partly under the pressure of secular ideology, partly in search of public moneys and curricular approval. From all of these adjustments to the demands of the world—to say nothing of liturgical and sacramental changes—it is evident that Christianity in Western liberal societies is in the process of shedding its sacred core and its external manifestations. Its ambition seems to be to dissolve itself in the prevailing ideology and to become indistinguishable from the desacralized milieu.

Ours is the first society in history that is emancipated from the sacred, in politics and by now in religion as well. The close interdependence of temple and palace needs no further demonstration. The decline of one brings in its wake the decline of the other, for the simple reason that *power must appear with the aura of the sacred*. As René Guénon notes, soon after political power emancipates itself from spiritual authority it loses its own stability and,

11. In Marxist countries, too, some churches have experimented with submission to the party and with acceptance of a place in "socialist society." Such a course has led to an impasse in each case; there is no reason why it should not lead to a similar impasse in the case of churches patterning themselves and their behavior on liberal postulates.

in short order, its legitimacy. The downward trend cannot be arrested. Individualism then anarchy appear as the natural consequence.[12] This was also the view of the Roman historians and of the Greek Polybius, the chronicler of Roman grandeur after the war with Carthage. The monarchy, they wrote, gave way to the government of a few, who unseated the king out of jealousy. This oligarchy was dispossessed in turn by a popular revolution, which brought the masses to power. Soon a generalized anarchy ensued, shored up again by quasi monarchs, the emperors who followed Caesar. We have no proof that such cycles have been broken.

In previous chapters we saw how first the temple then the palace lost what constituted their essential roots and character and how, when that happened, the religious was absorbed by the political, and subsequently the political by the landscape of indifference. The proliferation of laws, a substitute for tradition-sanctioned social relationships, merely dissimulates a state of permanent conflict, regarded as the principle of government and as the womb of social justice. Through the ever more complex network of laws—the delight of lawyers and bureaucratic regulators—citizens are attracted to, and actually practice, anarchy: they see no reason why the laws they are supposed to give to themselves as particles of popular sovereignty should be allowed to obstruct their instant satisfactions. Seen from the opposite end, from the perspective of those who govern, governing is reduced to confronting an endless series of ad hoc circumstances, each containing a potentially revolutionary and subversive program. To the citizens' anarchism the government reacts by multiplying its bureaucracies and committees. This too is a kind of anarchy, since there is no general design, either in domestic or foreign policy, by which these bureaucracies appear on the stage and are dismissed.

There is, of course, no enduring, stabilizing model for policy but typically only elections and referenda on new, temporary "models of society." Politics is gradually replaced by a feverishly managed futurology (I will discuss this further in Chapter Six)

12. Guénon, *Autorité spirituelle et pouvoir temporel* (Paris: Éditions Trédaniel, 1984), 43.

with the selection, on expert recommendation or under ideological pressure, of free-market models, authoritarian models, socialist models, military models, scientific-Marxist models, third world
models, or what have you. Usually, however, the model is not so
much chosen as imposed by a "strong man" who meets and shapes
circumstances. The personal and ideological element in model
making prompts a strong utopian current because politics appears
discredited, fragile, and shaped by pressure groups—party
bureaucracies, special interests, and intellectual fashions. Power
disappears somewhere in the resulting confusion. While it rises
now here now there in the midst of the fluctuations of the public,
it is everywhere fragmented and weak.

*   *   *

The United States' Protestant foundation is responsible for the permanent American search for a formula for seeing this country as
a religious moral community, a community of the elect. Underlying both the public and private debates are three major assumptions: (1) all other nations and societies are now and have been in
the past in various degrees immoral; some have been devilish, evil
empires; (2) only the United states was founded on a commitment
to God, a commitment strong enough even in this modernist century to lift Americans to a level of morality superior to the rest of
humanity; and (3) commitment to God in the political order consists in the advocacy of American social forms: democracy, pluralism, and the rule of the common citizen.

At first sight, one may conjecture that this society is thus
closest today of all worldly societies to the traditional model, a
society that regards itself as the earthly replica of the transcendent
pattern, carrying out the divine will. This ought to mean in turn
that the earlier analyses of this book about the sacred and its centrality for the phenomenon of power lose their validity and relevance on these shores. Indeed, Fr. John Courtney Murray, an eminent churchman who thought he could reconcile two traditions as
befits our ecumenicist age, attempted to demonstrate this view.
Murray's task, and that of many others before and after him, was
a considerable one since he had to legitimize by religious standards a political construct born in a Deistic-agnostic age and con-

ceived by men who were clearly stamped by Enlightenment ideology, including the Masonic doctrine.

The issue before the founding fathers and before Fr. Murray was a momentous one. The central practical problem for traditional kingdoms, from African tribal societies to medieval Christian empires, was that of continuity, since continuity is the concrete, mundane translation of the presence of the sacred. The fear of an interregnum, a suspension of continuity in which social cohesion loosens and authority breaks down, has haunted all societies to the present. Hence the many and rich symbols by which the ruler was identified with the body politic and the ruler's body itself seen as double: the mortal physical body and the much more important sacred body, which continues to hold power. Ernst Kantorowicz has explored the medieval formulation of this religiopolitical doctrine in his book *The King's Two Bodies,* and, more recently, anthropologist Georges Balandier has discussed its universal application.[13] The identification between the ruler's body and the political body always encouraged the corporeal allegory. In the old French monarchy, for example, continuity through change was indicated by the lowering of the flag at the moment the king died followed by its immediate reelevation, signifying that the new king was consecrated. "The king of France

---

13. Kantorowicz, *The King's Two Bodies: A Study in Mediaeval Political Theology* (Princeton: Princeton University Press, 1957); Georges Balandier, *Le détour, pouvoir et modernité* (Paris: Éditions Fayard, 1985). Kantorowicz quotes the following statement from an anonymous Norman tract, *De consecratione pontificum et regum* (c. 1100): "We thus have to recognize [in the king] a twin person, one descending from nature, the other from grace. . . . One through which, by the condition of nature, he conformed with other men; another through which, by the eminence of his deification and by the power of the sacrament [of consecration], he excelled all others. Concerning one personality, he was, by nature, an individual man; concerning his other personality, he was by Grace, a *Christus,* that is a God-man." Kantorowicz, *The King's Two Bodies,* 46. The doctrine of the "twin bodies" was deepened and applied particularly in England, though it was strong on the continent as well. Thus in the thirteenth century Cynus of Pistoia writes, "The emperor stems from the people; but the empire is from God, and because he presides over the empire, the emperor is called divine." Quoted in ibid., 103.

never dies!" was the saying. The royal continuity was uninterrupted and national unity assured.

The fear of the interregnum, for which so much blood was shed in both foreign and civil wars, was lifted by the concept of popular sovereignty. Rulers are mortal, but entire nations as such are not. Insofar as the people, the totality of the citizens, bear the sovereignty, dynastic continuity is no longer personalized, no longer problematical. Not even a symbolic moment of interregnum is then risked, because at the death of the ruler the people, directly or through representatives, appoint another one. Throughout, however, the people retain their ultimate sovereignty; the ruler is only a temporary carrier of borrowed power. This explains, it seems to me, why the electoral process is quasi-sacralized in modern democracies and why voting is strongly encouraged or even made compulsory: without voting an interregnum would actually be faced, and the "sovereign" would be found derelict in its duties. This is also why many in politics are so serious when they face the derision of their nondemocratic critics who point out the low participation of voters and the election of leaders by actual minorities. The democratic answer is that no matter how small the "majority" support of a candidate is (often not more than 25 or 30 percent of eligible voters), it embodies sovereignty and suffices as its voice.

For all these reasons, democracies need a (nonsacred) substitute for the sacred. Some say that this can be obtained by encouraging public debate and public participation in problem solving. This is, of course, in no sense a sacred procedure. In fact, it is a purely rational and at the same time conflictual procedure because democracy itself is founded on the untouchability of individuals and their interests, thus on their clashes. The act of voting replaces all the other sacred acts of politics; it is through the vote and its periodic (in some sense "ritual") repetition that the community becomes aware of itself and its power (its exercise of sovereignty). Through the instrumentality of the vote and the accompanying electoral campaign, politics—including the utterances and slogans of candidates, the race itself, and the proclamation of the winner—becomes the scene of the absorption of power in the assembled sovereign individuals, under whose aegis the permanent conflict is in a sense sacralized. Conflict is thus not feared as the interregnum used to be feared, even though it is, in a way, the reverse image of continuity. Hence the founding fathers decided that ephemeral and changing pressure groups (but are they really ephemeral?) would better secure the neutrality of political life than would permanent political parties. Their hope was that such groups would keep the inherent conflict closer to the level of the individual, while parties, they thought, would tend to institutionalize the clashes.

What Fr. Murray tried to grasp and formulate was the essence of a community *not* founded on the sacred. Quoting from the Declaration of Independence and Abraham Lincoln, he saw it founded on a *proposition*—"at once doctrinal and practical, a theorem and a problem"—in need of "intellectual assent" by successive generations and aiming at a "historical success."[14] This formula is quite the opposite of the foundation story of most other communities, which from the beginning of time have been searching for their legitimation in a cosmic-divine guarantee. The American foundation, however, sought evidence that would command intellectual assent: "We hold these truths to be self-evident. . . ." But this proposition, Murray adds, can never be finished: it is subject to continual reinterpretation, which requires a great deal of discipline and lucidity. Discipline is needed to remain inside the field of validity of the initial proposition; lucidity to measure the eventual deviations from the original meaning. Murray then correctly saw the need for political virtue—precisely this discipline and this lucidity—for the entire body of citizens, particularly for what he called the never-ending public argument by "informed men."

Indeed, what happens when one, two, or three centuries after the founding the original proposition and its proof are no longer seen as self-evident? If we read Murray attentively, we find that he takes temple and palace, the divinely legitimated agents of traditional societies, and replaces them in the American equation with intelligence (rational discourse) and government, that is, a bureaucracy which acts after deliberation and discourse. It is then

14. All quotations of Murray are from *We Hold These Truths* (London: Sheed & Ward, 1960).

to this bureaucracy, composed of thinking and deliberating people, that the task is confided to find "other, more reasoned grounds for their essential affirmation that [the American people] are uniquely a people, a free society." Otherwise, Murray adds, "the peril is great: the complete loss of identity, with all propriety of theological definition, is hell."

Even before such a somber prospect is envisaged, though, it is obvious that "public argument by informed men" is no substitute for the sacred guarantee. In the name of what authority would these men discipline themselves, as Murray's thesis proposes they would, if they totally reject reference to any sacred foundation? The lack of consensus in such a pluralistic society results not in polite argument but in discord, cacophony, and anarchy. Secular humanists, for example, do not agree at all with the semireligious inspiration of the initial proposition, although they in fact suggest a civic theology of their own. In order to arrive at even minimal agreement, the vestiges of state power with its residual sacred are jettisoned, and a kind of orderly anarchy, a conflictual civil society, is then installed as a loose framework containing (or restraining), more in appearance than in fact, the centrifugal tendencies.

One should therefore listen to what others write about the heart of this problem. The serious people in a pluralistic society who do sit down to discuss the question of a new consensus around the central proposition come from a variety of religious and moral backgrounds; thus insofar as the foundation of the proposition has a strong moral component, their views toward it may also strongly differ. Indeed, it is mainly in this that their "seriousness" consists, since the United States insists that its justification as a nation is a moral one. But as John A. Gueguen recently argued, "even people who seriously and sincerely sit down to reason out matters of public morality seem to read the moral nature of man, and hence the moral law of God, differently."[15]

The conflict that is embedded in the individualism of American society, as the various labels proposed by Irving Kristol suggest, will thus inevitably manifest itself at the very top, where Mur-

15. Gueguen, "Public Morality in Liberal Democracy," *Homiletic and Pastoral Review,* December 1985.

ray's "serious men" sit and deliberate about the continuity of the nation. It is conceivable, writes Gueguen, that one group may attempt "to drive the other from the field," that those who advocate democratic plurality, for example, may try to drive out those who stand for Christian morality. The two traditions may not have a common denominator. There are of course clashes even within Christian morality. The Reformation ethic, Gueguen continues, has tended to adapt Christian morality to the needs of civil society, while the Catholic ethic tends to adapt secular situations to the promotion of a truth about humanity by making these situations serve the moral imperatives found in the gospel.

Some argue that recent trends in Catholic thought show a desire to accommodate the Catholic minority to the Protestant majority. Others speak of the death of the Protestant era in America, the failure of the mainline denominations to exercise an authority capable of stemming the nation's slide into neopaganism. Yet hardly anybody discusses the underlying causes of such decay, let alone the consequences, since the public rhetoric still attributes the American "success story" to the observance of God's laws. The "death of God" theme is forbidden on the political forum even though it has become a substantial, if not the dominant, influence in our universities, literature, and intellectual discourse.

The nondiscussion which lies heavily in the atmosphere around us has so far concealed the fact that American society and Western society in general is now at the end of a long tradition, but that it is a deviant from it. The tradition held that political power is inseparable from spiritual authority, the former depending on the latter whose consecration is indispensable for legitimacy and public order. Now, unlegitimized political power does not necessarily collapse but it becomes fragmented and contested, first by the equally large power concentrations of civil society (business, labor, the news media, the intellectual establishment, various other bureaucracies) then by the anarchic tendencies inherent in individualism. At a certain point, power is no longer exercised except in the form of bureaucratic measures—a kind of traffic-light authority. Great national decisions are consequently blocked—sometimes by open opposition, to be sure, but also by the skepticism and cynicism of those who hold power.

Recent confirmation of this comes from an unexpected quarter. A report by the Brookings Institution, "Religion in American Public Life" (1985), states that "in a democratic society, persons subscribing to a classical humanist ethics are driven to hypocrisy and cynicism—either pretending admiration or fellow-feeling for the masses that their value system does not sustain, or scorning the political forms under which they live. In either case, social bitterness between humanist elites and the mass of working-class and middle-class citizens is bound to follow." Even more important is the report's observation that the banishment of religion does not create a neutral field in which religion and secularism may coexist; one is always bound to win out in the end. To conduct public institutions without any acknowledgement of religion is simply secularism. Yet civil society's moral and political well-being depends on an ultimately transcendent direction, the report says. "Social authority is legitimized by making it answerable to transcendent moral law."

These surprisingly lucid statements may themselves support a temporary political-cultural opportunism, but they may also herald a profounder search into the presuppositions of political power. As such, they may become a part of the deliberations of the "serious men" dedicated to thinking about Fr. Murray's proposition. The question is whether "deliberations," precisely because they touch only one's rational faculties, can tackle such problems as political power. Balandier mentions that modern anthropology focuses on the regular and consecrated practices of societies that guarantee cohesion through the rituals of reviving the old order as the source of power. Thus tradition, order, ritual, and power are again seen by some—as they were seen by every society preceding ours—as necessarily connected realities. In contrast, redefining with every new generation a nation's central inspiration and foundation may be the ideal only of those who support the social contract theory and of those who regard political power as an evil to be eliminated from history. These views originate in the liberal dogma of individualism, which today is responsible for the fragility of Western societies and their miscomprehension of power.

Fr. Yves Congar, the theologian criticised for his modernist views by Pius XII in 1950, formulated the issue cogently when he wrote, apropos of *dignitatis humanae,* the religious freedom clause of the Second Vatican Council: "The novelty of this doctrine is that it bases freedom not in the objective moral truth, but in the ontological quality of the human person."[16] With this shift, individuals are recognized as intrinsically free, not obligated to listen to or obey a source of authority outside themselves, either in the moral area or, consequently, in the political area. People thus emancipated do not tolerate authority and power above them and ultimately undermine the social nexus. Because of the doctrinal switch evident in *dignitatis humanae,* Congar called Vatican II "The Church's October Revolution." It might more appropriately be called its "Kantian revolution," since Kant rooted morality in the ethical consciousness of the individual. What Congar diagnoses is nothing less than the foundation of "liberation theology."

These remarks about the Catholic church's aggiornamento have their place in the reflection on the American deliberations by serious people. Giving new content to the proposition on which the country was founded and to the truths we hold to be self-evident is a demarche similar to the rethinking nowadays of Catholic doctrine by every council, as well as by those minicouncils held by gatherings of theologians and by episcopal conferences and other bodies distancing themselves from Rome. In fact, what I have said so far about individualism, the conflictual society, the variations of the consensus, and the serious thinkers with different backgrounds and ideologies seems also to be astonishingly true of the two Western Christian institutions, the Catholic and Protestant churches. In the last half-century, temporal and spiritual power have been been rapidly undermining their own foundations, as though locked in a race to see which one is able to do it faster and more thoroughly. In recent decades a kind of cultural power has consequently emerged—spreading worldwide from its focus in America—which openly derides and flaunts power as only a countersociety or counterculture would.

It is interesting to note that traditional societies too reserved a place for the subversion of order. They set aside various feast days for the rule of disorder, during which slaves and outcasts (today's

16. Congar, writing in *Etudes et Documents,* no. 5 (15 June 1965): 5.

"marginals") held court, shaming and ridiculing the holders of power and their authority. In Rome, the period was the Saturnalia, with habits and costumes passed on to Christianity (to reappear during Mardi Gras). The medieval kings had their clowns, a kind of "third body" of the ruler who imitated and made fun of him and who, in this comic disguise, was expected to be a commentator on the ruler's acts, words, and behavior—a source of caricature through which the ruler could contemplate his own mirror image.

These semiofficial representatives of the countersociety were, however, *inside* the sacred dimension of power. Not only was their freedom relative and limited in time, but the Saturnalia crowds and the king's clown acted out a certain prescribed role. They represented the profane, the desacralized, the other face of the human condition. Over against the self-image of the community—of both ruler and subjects—the clown functioned as the outsider, perilously edging toward the scapegoat. Indeed, his punishment or humiliation could be cruel. In the process, the essential sacrality of the community could be reaffirmed.

The loss of the sacred and of sacralized power in our political societies, by contrast, may be diagnosed as the sacralization of the counterculture, which has now become the accepted model for "official" society to follow and recognize as a superior form. It is better to speak here of culture than of society because the latter is structurally in disarray through the permanent clashes tearing at its entrails. Culture, on the other hand, is today the only acknowledged public arena in which the masses and their entertainers meet outside the conflicts and propose worldviews not indebted to past or future, to knowledge or taste, to any effort or superior achievement. Culture represents, like the Roman Saturnalia, an unassailable domain, a terra incognita on society's map where anything is allowed as long as it scoffs at reason, symbols, respected values, common sense, and moral decency. Thus "culture power" is the only recognizable power that does not hide and wears no mask. It occupies the throne evacuated by the ruler, but only to desecrate it, to show its irrelevance—the clown not only imitates the king, he has taken his place.

Culture has come to mean, of course, anything that happens to catch the fancy of a group: rock concerts supposedly for the famished of the third world; the drug culture and other subcultures; sects and cults; sexual excess and aberration; blasphemy on stage and screen; frightening and obscene shapes; the plastic wrapping of the Pont-Neuf or the California coast; the smashing of the family and other institutions; the display of the queer, the abject, the sick. These instant products, meant to provide instant satisfaction to a society itself unmoored from foundation and tradition, accordingly deny the work of mediation and maturation and favor the incoherent, the shapeless and the repulsive. But before we discount this culture as insignificant, we must ask ourselves whether it is not the last stage of individualism and whether it therefore lies now within the logic of our societies. If it remains free to expand in time and space, if the official but intimidated spokesmen of the political body give it their consent, if it spreads out in moviehouse, museum, festival, press, and university, the reason may be that it embodies society's ideal, the ideal that Fr. Murray's serious men can no longer satisfy with their political deliberations.

It seems evident, then, that in a community in which the antisacred and the counterculture, far from being marginalized, have become the admired forms of expression, power cannot be exercised and certainly not comprehended. Self-expression, a revealing term, opposes the concept of the collective body whose metaphors filled the annals of traditional societies. Instead of recognizing itself as a body—in fact, the incarnation of an archetype—modern society with its willed and accepted conflicts and its counterculture appears as a disordered machine whose parts work out surrealistically their various whims.[17] Power itself goes into hiding behind innocent-sounding facades: it is exercised—but without the appropriate label—by the party secretary, the busi-

17. It may not be an error to attribute the popularity of "socialism" and the almost mystical aura which surrounds the term to the need to imagine the opposite of liberal "anarchy." Socialism is thus widely credited with the ability to restore the community as a nexus and network which is more simple than liberal society and in which this simplicity is brought about by concentrating much of the power in the hands of the state. Conflicts based on cash relations would disappear, the disciples of socialism hold, and culture would reflect human realities. It is another story that socialism in action betrays all these expectations.

ness executive, the anchorman on television, the labor leader, the team of a brain trust or a think tank. Metaphors of camouflaged power have nothing to do with the community as a body but only with special or ideological interests. The reason is evident. In a body the parts work for their mutual benefit, they constitute an organic whole, they are associated for a finality. Nothing like it exists in modern society whose members work at cross-purposes. Hence they are not distinguished from each other. The energy input of their clashes is the more potent as the parts are more uniform. This is called "equality"; indeed, the passion of conflict and envy is strongest when the contenders are equal.

Marcel Gauchet proclaims that the society of the future will be postreligious, that it will have overthrown the structures inspired by religious faith. Yet he suggests that such a situation is compatible with islands of intense religiosity. For reasons given in this and other chapters, I am of the opinion that Gauchet speaks less of a still-hypothetical future than of what he experiences around him in all Western nations. We may also extend his observation on the status of religion to the status of power: they are both desacralized. There are concentrations of power in our society just as there are centers of spirituality, yet society at large functions in the main avenues without any structured and structuring power, and it passes the pockets by.

While faith is an internal matter that may subsist, even flourish, without the institutional forms of religion, power cannot exist outside of institutional forms—ultimately, without the state—or there can be no community. There may be bands with an intense cohesion around a charismatic leader, but there can be no articulated community without a power structure, an acknowledged hierarchy, and an external, cosmic or divine agent that confers meaning to the whole. We are thus approaching societies without the sacred and without power. To use the words of Gauchet again, the political enterprise is no longer justified in calling itself the concretization of the heavenly law. Political power is subverted in its symbolic foundation and sacred identity. Its roots, hence its mediating legitimacy, have been removed by a quiet revolution. Liberal democracy has proved to be the passage from society founded on the sacred to society founded on nothing but itself.

I have said above that the weakening of the state in the West has allowed gigantic pressure groups to emerge which use power in a noninstitutionalized, thus naked, form but whose nakedness is camouflaged by a high-sounding vocabulary. We have "friendly banks," "academic families," "truth-seeking media," a "morally indignant public opinion," and so on. In all these matters, the communist system seems to present a caricature of the Western state of affairs as well as an alternative form of power. Under the Soviet system, for example, power says out loud what in the West it tries to neutralize or embellish. This is because the Soviet world, rid of the last vestiges of the divine, displays the mundane dimension as an end in itself, the focus of all possible imagination and conception. The state is not a mediating agent placed between the cosmos and the citizens; it is itself the source of the sacred as the only existent, the true reality. This is the root of what we call *totalitarianism,* a term generally misinterpreted and incorrectly used. For if the essence of totalitarianism were to be unmasked, one would have to acknowledge that it does not consist in the cancerous growth of the state but rather in the elimination from the state of its role as a mediator of transcendence. Such a statement goes against the grain of those who see in the state a mere service station, an arrangement of mere convenience, or even an enemy of civil society, though indeed a necessary evil.

Our observation of power today shows its atrophy in the Western democracies and hypertrophy in communist countries. In spite of this apparent contrast, the common basis of the two systems cannot be denied. In both, the *worldly* has acquired an unquestioned autonomy and exclusivity, which translates in the political order as the nonrecognition of the community's meaning derived from an outside transcendent source. The community cannot, however, give meaning to itself, and Fr. Murray's thesis that such a meaning may periodically be reexamined and rediscussed is, to say the least, naive. Only the sixth sense, the spiritual one, is able to recognize that nations and societies are linked to a meaning-conferring source, and that a certain hierarchy translates it into the language of mundane reality. Only in such a way is the community permeated by the consciousness of a spiritual-moral order to which the political order remains attached.

The negation of the moral reality plainly leads to the dissolution of the civic order because the citizens cease to detect behind the one and the other an unquestioned cosmic-divine reality. In the West, the indispensable spiritual vision is obstructed by the consumer society and its ever-growing pyramids of objects and images. The glut chokes the senses and discourages the spirit, particularly as the piled-up goods, pictures, and slogans are presented as a guarantee of freedom, a protection against servitude. In the Marxist system, the spiritual vision is confounded by the monolithic social structure, and the citizens are choked by laws against expressing the soul's elementary aspirations. In both systems, each of which celebrates the abolition of extramundane meaning, what used to be political power becomes indistinguishable from the mechanical motions of a vast, impersonal apparatus.

It is instructive to reflect upon the great transformation the concept of the state and power has undergone in the last several centuries. In the sacralized milieu, inherited from previous ages and continued uninterruptedly, the church's hierarchical body was the prototype of monarchies—to such an extent that the state had come to be regarded as a *corpus mysticum,* and its governing formulas sought to imitate those of Christian liturgy.[18] God's presence took shape as strong institutions both in the political hierarchy and in the law-giving process. Today we witness a completely different situation. The prototype is a functioning machine, and relationships in society are mechanical ones. The ever-present danger of social conflicts (mechanical breakdowns), which immediately affect tens of millions, inhibits power and silences any claim that power derives from a transcendent source. The holders of power are thus like engineers of a locomotive or pilots of a giant airplane: they set the machine into motion but are not responsible for what is inside the machine and how the many parts are affected by turning the ignition key. When the mechanism no longer responds, some parts are repaired or the whole is replaced by a similarly unknown, impersonal mechanism. The holders of power become themselves part of the machine. They are quite different

18. Kantorowicz, *Mourir pour la patrie* (Paris: Presses Universitaires de France, 1984), 86, 137. This volume contains excerpts from *The King's Two Bodies.*

from the power holders in traditional society, who are mediators. As Jean Brun remarks of modern human beings, they are no longer understood as subjects linked to transcendence but as objects knowable from outside—the only dimension that matters— manipulable by the world in which they are integrated.[19]

*   *   *

Why is it, then, that our societies still function, that myriad tasks get performed as surely as the sun rises, and that cohesion and loyalty everyday overcome the forces of disaffection, cynicism, and hostility? This is just one variation on the timeless political question: Why is there command and obedience? Why do the many submit to the few? Why is there a political structure instead of a universal and permanent anarchy?

I shall not review here the multitude of answers given by modern sociologists, philosophers, and social engineers whose reasoning is so often circular: sociability, group interest, fear, conformism, contract, lack of independent thinking, and the list goes on. My first answer is, rather, that every society contains self-perpetuating elements crystallized around routine tasks which then result, almost automatically, in an ever-widening network of tasks, each predicated on the regular performance of the others. This is true of every society; it is almost a biological precondition.

My second answer, pertaining only to our modern societies, depends on the concept of popular sovereignty, by which, as we saw, the sacralization of continuity has been replaced by the sacralization of conflict. To use Alexandre Koyré's terminology, the "closed cosmos" used to be continuous, ruled by familiar forces and the scene of interactions between macrocosm and microcosm. The "infinite universe," in contrast, is characterized only by meaningless motions; it is on a permanent collision course, heading (if that is the right word) toward the unknown. In traditional society, discontinuity—especially the interruption of dynastic permanence—was allowed only at great risk. Meticulous precision was observed in ritual, because the myriad influences and affinities which composed the cosmos had to be properly dealt with

---

19. Brun, *L'homme et le langage* (Paris: Presses Universitaires de France, 1985), 119.

(pacified, neutralized, won over) to ensure the smooth continuity of community affairs. Modern society feels safe in its dependence on itself alone and exalts its freedom of creating and solving conflicts on a purely human level. Although it does not possess traditional society's familiarity with the cosmos, it feels it has seen through the universe by giving it unchanging, mechanical laws.

Yet, at the same time, modern society is dimly aware of its own fragility and ephemeral character. The conflicts and collisions put in question the resistance of the social tissue, because each conflict reverberates through the entire mechanism, creating resentment and hostility that cannot be absorbed.[20] The resulting growth and strength of centrifugal forces challenge social cohesion, preventing the sacralization of anything but "freedom," a sacralization pregnant with only more conflict. Conflict solving, which ought to be the task of strong institutions, and only in the last analysis that of the state, is weakened by the tacit injunction of individualistic liberalism against strong institutions. Over and over again, the state itself is rocked and the common good is shown as irrelevant.[21] Power itself continually diminishes since it must hide behind a symbolless anonymity and cannot be sacralized. Churches no longer project a spiritual authority, as we have seen. At best, they refer to vague "moral values" in no way distinct from "democratic civic values"; at worst, they adopt the language and the slogans of fashionable ideologies.[22]

Numerous writers have suggested that the vanished sacred foundation of the state and of political power has yielded to a ra-

20. Recall the words of the Brookings Institute's report, p. 112 above.

21. Instances of this include strikes, racial strife, class struggles, party rivalries, and conflicts between instantly ideologized and politicized ad hoc groups.

22. A recent article by Cardinal Franz König of Austria may serve as an illustration. Containing not a word about spirituality and salvation, the text repeats the clichés uttered at international congresses of disarmament, unemployment, neocolonialism, and so on. These recommendations are no longer just banal, their repetition demoralizes the imagination and goodwill of more original minds. They make it sound as if the church had been founded as a shadow cabinet for temporal authorities, with departments of agriculture, defense, industry, and foreign affairs. Meanwhile, the authentically spiritual religious voice remains silent.

tional insight which accepts the state and power on other than "mythological" grounds.[23] The state must exist, these writers hold, even though it is a "curse." Without it there is no legitimacy, no conflict resolution. These writers then cautiously approach the issue of a resacralization—not because they posit a transcendence but because they want to save civil society's orderly procedures. They raise the question of an "immanent sacred" compatible with modernity. We shall see in the next chapter whether this is a viable option.

23. This is the thesis of Georges Burdeau, for example, in *L'Etat* (Paris: Éditions du Seuil, 1970), 78.

CHAPTER SIX

The Restoration of the Sacred

As we made a tour of the sacred in a few selected areas of its manifestation—religion, political power, and art—we also had the opportunity to measure the distance that the modern world has traveled from the religious, political, and artistic forms in which the sacred used to be embedded. Throughout the ages, the sacred has not been confined to museum pieces, to an ancient drinking cup or an exotic headmask adorning a dusty shelf; it was rather alive and fully active in human culture, the central reality permeating civilizations. It infused the artistic and poetic imagination; it nourished religious worship and the cult, calling forth veneration and awe; it was present in political ritual and was intimately linked to the exercise of power. The sacred was tied to persons, objects, and events, and also, above all, to the past—to immutability, to distance, and to the ritual repetition of fixed words and acts. The sacred was brought home to members of the community at all levels; it explained the significance of the cosmos, architecture, and social institutions.

The universality of the sacred and its unbroken presence in some cultural contexts explain why those inside its world do not actually apprehend its presence, just as they hardly notice ordinary habitual occurrences. For the same reason, members of a desacralized civilization—our civilization—are not aware that practically all reference to the sacred has been erased from our daily existence.[1]

1. One can perhaps gain such an awareness by traveling in foreign cultures. I became very much conscious, in Islamic, Hindu, and Confucian cultures, of their vast differences from Christian presuppositions, structures of

To those who notice and wonder, this appears as a natural phenomenon, and they satisfy their short-lived quest for the sacred with the conclusion that evolution, progress, humanity's maturity, or some other "mutation" or "qualitative leap" into absolute novelty has replaced the centrality of the sacred with the ubiquity of *culture*. The functions of the two—the traditional sacred and modern culture—are then seen as identical: both are supposed merely to represent the means allowing us to switch from the workaday world of routine to leisure and relaxation. Attending church and attending a concert have become practically equivalent excursions into the leisure-culture continuum.

The belief in the equivalence of the products of our "culture industry" and of the sacred is promoted by the modern cult of science. Not only is science perceived as the quintessence of modernity, it also responds to our aspiration to possess a form of the inexplicable and mysterious, which, instead of focusing on the past, focuses on the future. In other respects, too, science conforms to what modern people expect: it seems to be a level above the daily routine, yet it also penetrates that routine. In other words, people today look to science with expectations similar to those they always had of the sacred. In modern existence, science, together with its applications in technology, plays the role that the sacred used to play in traditional societies: it is ever-present, it fires and satisfies the imagination, it provokes awe and reverence, and it dictates a certain ritual behavior.

While these features would seem to qualify science as the new sacred, they are more than balanced by others which disqualify it from becoming sacralized. One could, of course, argue that the scientific order that modernity perceives in the universe is built on more solid ground than that on which the sacred order rested. Our ability to predict the arrival of a comet or the cooling off of a star is far more precise than the exploration and manipulation of celestial and occult influences by magical means. What is missing from

---

thinking, and values. Similarly, travel in countries under communist regimes makes one attentive to the absence of a religious culture, or at least of its authorized public manifestations. From such a distance, travelers may become aware of the temporary absence of their own spiritual grounding, and of the presence of another sacred meaning in place, time, and conduct.

the calculations and forecasts of science, however, is what humanity craves above all: the immutability of vision explained by the
intentions and workings of a superhuman consciousness, that is,
by cosmic impulses, levels of being, the division of the world into
sacred and profane. We may appropriately quote the words of Titus
Burckhardt here as they convey human expectations: "Architecture is a synthesis of the world: what in the universe is in incessant motion, sacred architecture transposes into permanent
forms."[2] This remark brings into focus something essential: the
desire to capture infinity in a reduced and concentrated form
without, however, losing its original power. Again, we see the in-
separability of macrocosm and microcosm.

But can infinity be captured in a *scientific* formula? Unlike a
sacred form of architecture, Einstein's equation $E = mc^2$ has no
power of penetrating the senses, the imagination, or the soul; it
possesses no existential dimensions and does not call forth
veneration. Within the framework of sacrality it is not "real," or
at least its reality does not affect us in depth. No cult may be built
around it, and while the formula may be valid in all known circumstances, it is rendered fragile and ephemeral by our expecta-
tion that tomorrow another scientist may find a more inclusive,
hence more "real," formulation—as indeed the theory of relativity is more inclusive than Newton's laws. A sacred cultic formula,
in contrast, burns itself into the believer's soul by its content and
its transcendent reference, as well as by rhythmic repetition
through which words and gestures from the past are made to live
again, exercising their impact at all time. No change of validity
affects it.

In consequence, science, which occupies a place of honor
among the modern candidates to the sacred, hardly begins to qualify for that role.[3] The other candidates are disqualified as well be-

2. Burckhardt, *Principes et méthodes de l'art sacré* (Paris: Dervy
Livres, 1976), 18.

3. True, Isaac Newton still believed that "this most beautiful system of
the sun, planets, and comets" was not to be attributed to "some blind
metaphysical necessity, but could only proceed from the counsel and dominion of an intelligent and powerful Being" (quoted in Jaroslav Pelikan,
Jesus through the Centuries [New Haven: Yale University Press, 1985],

cause they cannot identify themselves with the transcendent any more than can science, any more than can any object or person chosen at random. We human beings are directed toward the sacred by the unerring insight that our innermost core is an imageless image of the center of being. St. Augustine expressed this by saying that God was nearer his soul than he himself was. One cannot, for mere human convenience, designate a phenomenon as sacred; sacrality cannot be attributed simply to popularly acclaimed objects, no matter how widely recognized and admired. The present century is, of course, particularly tempted to do just that, since, with the help of technology, sensational images can be projected worldwide. A world of wonders appears on the television screen, sex symbols have millions of viewers, spectacular successes from sports to space navigation flash simultaneously in every home. There is no lack of striking formulas and envied objects, yet it is evident that such one-dimensional and ephemeral appearances belong to the sphere of the profane.

It is nonetheless natural that our contemporaries maintain the search for new sacred forms which would ground their being. We are so elated by the incomparable achievements of modernity that we regard it as an offense that we have not yet produced the sacred or its perfect imitation. The best writers, thinkers, and artists are especially embarrassed by the complete desacralization around them, sensing deep down that their own achievements are devalued without spiritual foundations stabilizing their milieu. In consequence, many make desperate but aborted efforts to locate a new sacred, a transcendental source. Quite appropriately, people seek the sacred mainly in the two areas where they (without necessarily admitting it) miss it most, and where its conspicuous absence reveals a scandalous vacuum: in religion and politics. Yet here an insurmountable contradiction arises, namely, the belief that the "modern sacred" ought to have a degree of scientific verifiability. As a result, certain modern myths arise—in truth

---

183). But Newton's view, still compatible with the sacralization of science, has since yielded to the prevalent theories of today, exemplified by Jacques Monod's *Le hasard et la nécessité,* in which life and spirit are explained through the interaction of chance and determinism.

seedbeds of ideologies—offering themselves as frameworks for endlessly variable contents.

Five such ideological constructs have held this century's fancy because they were able to combine science and myth in a speculative manner. These are the dialectics of master and slave (Hegel); permanent evolution from lower to higher forms (Darwin); the abolition of social class resulting in the workers' paradise (Marx); the death of God and the rise of the Superman (Nietzsche); and the Oedipal murder of a father by his incestuous son (Freud). A cursory examination of these modern myths points to two recurring characteristics. The first is that each aims at the overthrow of the superior form (master, human being, bourgeoisie, God, dominant father) in favor of the inferior (slave, undeveloped form, proletariat, Superman, child), thus revealing the current inferior as the "dialectical" superior. This line of mythical speculation led to the revolutions of our time, feeding them with emotion and scientific optimism. A more important characteristic in the end is the radical disendowment of the past with its religious and political structure and the exaltation of the future as the milieu in which a new humanity and a new reality will finally come into their own. The old assumptions will be liquidated and considered only as historical curios, abandoned signposts on the way to self-fulfillment and new potentialities.

These modern myths, each in its own way but also lending support to the others, are lines of search for a sacred grounding in our disoriented times. By transferring reality's center from the three-dimensional time structure—past, present, future—to the future alone as the only valid dimension, time itself is speculatively abolished, and future becomes an unstructured "timeless time." What traditional humanity calls history and the concrete preoccupation with the present, the new myth makers regard as a mere preparation for the new humanity's true fulfillment localized in an ideal and happy permanence—utopia. To use Mircea Eliade's diagnosis, the new myths—or, rather, the mythic basis on which ideologies feed—aim at relieving humanity of the "terror of history," that is, of the always incalculable consequences of human interactions. They then replace it with an immanent paradise, without conflict in history, society, and the psyche. The preeminent philosophical expression of this demiurgic enterprise is that of Nietzsche, who undertook to endow the future with the relevance and prestige and with the weight and sacrality until now reserved for the past, so that humankind might tilt toward a new human condition.[4] This is nothing less than the attempted sacralization of the future, a process continuing in our days as well, even though the epigones of Nietzsche and the other mythmakers lack the master's overarching imaginative genius and content themselves with the elaboration of various prosaic futurologies.[5]

With the theoretical constructs of Hegel, Nietzsche, and Freud, among others, the traditional sacred dropped out of relevance. The processes it required have been reversed. Gone are immutability, the mediation of transcendent reality to a mundane replica, and the repetitive rituals reenacting the link to the model—all of them characteristic of the past and its evocation. In their place the future-as-sacred mythologies offer new configurations, spectacular changes, and the sense of conquest. What is more, these are all under human control.[6] The element of repetition in the sacred dimension was a punctilious rehearsal of past events and significances; thus each rehearsal added weight to permanence. Such re-

4. Nietzsche's philosophical aspiration can be summed up in his own words: "The thing to do is to endow *becoming* with the character of *being*. . . . This is the ultimate form of the will to power." *Will to Power,* II, no. 170.

5. The epigones of these mythmakers oversimplify and banalize the bold though erroneous concepts of their masters. Sartre has "corrected" Marx by existentialism; James Hillman has reduced Jung's explorations of the psyche to a primitive version of polytheism; René Girard has reformulated the Freudian thesis as the doctrine of violence, the founding act of the community; Marcuse has combined Freud's pansexuality and Marx's classless society to create the "liberated communes" of California; Teilhard de Chardin has "Christianized" Darwin to indicate a "hominization" and finally a "Christification" of the cosmos at Point Omega. The epigones of Nietzsche, perhaps the greatest mythmaker of all, cannot be counted. Let me add that I understand by "modern mythmaking" a false presentation of the human condition for ideological purposes. The Platonic myths are not artificially fabricated like Freud's and Marx's, for they translate the soul's permanent movement between the human and the divine.

6. Compare this view with the discussion of the "conflictual society" in Chapter Four.

petition permeated the better part of the religious and political scene and was reflected in art, law, education, and social institutions. The center of cosmic gravity was located in the past and its evocations, and even the future was imagined on that pattern. The sacralization of the future thus represents a displacement of humanity's collective thrust and meaning. While the meaning of the past lies in the ordering of all things for eternity by an eternal being, the meaning of the future engages reflection and imagination in the opposite direction: it entrusts science, not religion, with the rearrangement of things according to new orders and disorders.

We witness, in short, the replacement of the transcendent order by the future, therefore the replacement of the divine communication through the sacred by the human arrangements of societal forms. This may be a valid undertaking from a purely intellectual point of view because it is seen as preserving some semblance of the traditional sacred and it allows a transposition of the social cohesion of the past to our "naked public square."[7] In other words, our contemporary thinkers—by no means the mythmakers alone—believe that a radical break has already been effected in the religious and political continuum and that the immediate task is for thoughtful and responsible people to devise a political and social order *without* the sacred component, although with the benefit of scientific discoveries. It is fascinating to watch good minds devote their best efforts to this task and agree on a new philosophical anthropology founded on humanity's scientific and technical abilities.

This "postmodern" enterprise consists in an anxiety-filled exploration of the limits of the human condition. Modernity had led us to assume no limits to our Promethean aspirations and capabilities. A more sober postmodernity, however, perceives humanity as enclosed within a structure which may only yield to another, no less limited, structure. True, the sacred is inscribed in most of these structures (in those of Jung, Eliade, and Girard, and in those of modern anthropologists, psychologists, historians, and mythographers—see Chapter One), but its independence of humanity is

7. The phrase is Richard Neuhaus's, from his book *The Naked Public Square: Religion and Democracy in America* (Grand Rapids: Eerdmans, 1984).

denied—at times uncomfortably, but denied nevertheless. The problem before our thinkers is thus how to imagine and formulate better and wider structures; how to endow humanity with faculties of generating its own sacred, its own cohesive communities. The (reformulated) sacred ought to have some function in the community, but preferably on a reduced scale and with a low intensity. True, anthropologists today do insist that regular and ritualized practices are essential for human groups to maintain order and provide a recognized foundation for power; yet they argue that only on a lower level of evolution did people need the centrality of the sacred and its mediation of transcendence. Mature humanity has evolved beyond this stage, they say; human beings are now able to govern themselves with a different kind of sacred, within which they make their own basic decisions.

What is the shape of this trust in human power? Fundamentally, the confidence rests on human insights gained through technology, psychology, and democracy. It is tempered, paradoxically, by the additional insight that these achievements do not deliver the key to absolute domination and absolute happiness. The new wisdom, as its proponents like to call it (the French philosopher Raymond Ruyer calls it "the Princeton Gnosis"), suggests that achievements are not limitless in any one area or any one dimension and that we must pay a price for them because at any point they may turn against us who had invented or harmonized them or set them in motion. While we no longer speak of the sacred as belonging to the transcendent, we feel that the structure of the universe is such that a forever elusive law prevents our complete grasp and domination of it. Thus a more modest vision and approach are in order than what modernity had authorized—not because a personal God or cosmic symmetries impose choices, rewards, and punishments, but because domination over the outside world and ourselves quickly reaches obstacles, unexpected reverberations, and counterproductive results.[8]

8. A school of thought in sociology initiated by Ivan Illich propagates the view that modern technology and sociocultural progress bring regression or destruction in proportion to their own achievements. The more cars are manufactured, the slower the traffic on our highways; the more children are admitted to school, the lower the level of education.

Since humanity is forced back on its own resources (the post-modern vision), we must reinvent ourselves and arrange our world as our only habitat. This is exactly what existentialism teaches, without the Marxist element that distorts its Sartrean version. The German existentialist Michael Landmann writes, for example, that no image of humanity is true since all are historically conditioned; therefore all we can do is point out "man's openness and postulate his completion." As maker of one's own image, Landmann believes, one becomes a *creatura creatrix* (literally, a "creature able to create," or, better, a "godlike creator"). We read similar views in a recent book by Hans Jonas, who proposes a new anthropology with a reasoned image of humanity, new principles for human conduct, and a new self-governance in our search into the nature of things.[9] Both writers have sobered from the utopian goals of the last several generations but have merely fallen back on hopes for a new cognitive and emotional education.

It is rather clear that these and other thinkers are motivated by distrust of technology and of the uses to which certain human predispositions can put it, such as the total state, wholesale consumerism, hedonistic morality, violence, and depersonalization. They would like therefore to strengthen humanity qua humanity, in the hopes that we can learn to cope with all the powers we have unleashed. The "ethical individual" and the "responsible public person" are thus entrusted with the task of keeping themselves at an equal distance from all the threats that this century has presented. What these thinkers do not contemplate in these quasi-therapeutic approaches to modernity is that human beings are not Prometheus; they offer an extremely frail ground on which to reconstruct the community. Calling human beings ethical individuals and *creatura creatrix* may remind them of their moral nature, but it will also make them forget what is needed to be moral, namely, external support from institutional compulsion, religious imperatives, or the coercive apparatus of law and state—all of them performing only when sacralized.

A good illustration of this is offered in Richard Neuhaus's recent book, *The Naked Public Square*. While Landmann, Jonas, and

9. Jonas, *The Imperative of Responsibility: In Search of an Ethics for the Technological Age* (Chicago: University of Chicago Press, 1984).

others are prompted by puzzlement and disappointment over the impasse of Western religion and morality, Neuhaus is more focused. He is astonished and disturbed by the turn that American society has taken under the impact of modernity. America and the modern world—the former as the showcase of the latter— have been linked in the imagination of two centuries; as much hope has been attached to the one as to the other. Together they were expected to overcome the burden of the past and work out new realities in religion, politics, prosperity, and happiness.

Neuhaus finds, however, not only a conflict-ridden America but also the indication that the evidences on which the nation was founded are now questioned and rejected, possibly by a majority of the population if we add up the two "extremes" that the author discusses as "left" and "right."[10] Between the two forces, both of which mix religion and politics, Neuhaus chances upon the "naked public square," that is, a desacralized society. He believes that with such a neutral center America cannot survive. From its earlier attachment to the divine, American religion has rapidly narrowed its scope to the sole ideal of "freedom," not only as a means of achieving worthy objectives but indeed as an objective in itself. Technological anarchy and the aimless life against which Hans Jonas warns have become, in the eyes of citizens and institutions, just as valid social goals as the morally good life because we lack an arbiter to judge the superiority of one over the other. Neuhaus correctly concludes that the American polity is naked and purposeless.

Yet he shies away from a rededication to the sacred. In fact, he thinks that if those with a religious view accepted a moderation of their claims and a degree of liberalization, religion would have a good chance of "clothing" the nakedness of the public square. Not only is this an unrealistic demand to make of an admittedly politicized religion, but Neuhaus's position also leads to the same impasse as that of the other writers I have discussed. He too is intent on formulating a substitute sacred which would be compatible with the present ideology of the public square, that is, with the primacy of the pluralist status quo. Even if his project materialized,

10. Note the similarity of Neuhaus's probe to the questions raised by Fr. John Courtney Murray (see Chapter Five).

the religious component shorn of its transcendent vocation would bring a new confirmation to society's favorable vision of itself.

In other societies of the West, where democracy was never "articulated as a credal cause" (Neuhaus's felicitous phrase about Jeffersonian and Jacksonian America), the problem is not posed in any different terms. There too reflective thinkers are to seek a formula by which individuals and society as a whole could perform approximately the same functions they did in traditional ages—but now without the sacred whose indispensable centrality these thinkers refuse to envisage. Georges Burdeau writes, for example, that the ordinary citizen assumes the existence of some (transcendent) power behind the decisions of those who govern but cannot accredit the "fables, miracles, and other sacralizations" that used to surround the manifestations of power in the past. The ordinary citizen requires a "rational intellectual construct" in the place of "mythology." As a consequence, the idea of the state— by which Burdeau understands (one wonders why) a post-Renaissance institution—has come to replace "the mysterious forces which, in magical thought, used to dominate the powerholders' minds. Thus the concept of the state makes power acceptable."[11]

This is truncated argumentation. The reason why the state used to command a more intense loyalty and display a greater cohesion was precisely because it stood under the protection of the sacred and acknowledged its own sacred origins. It is questionable—as Neuhaus's work shows—whether a nonsacralized power can function in the long run when its promises (of science, technology, social theory, etc.) are found illusory. Indeed, what Burdeau's arguments suggest is a search for compromise: the future as the dominant category and orientation of life has cleansed the mind of mysteries, miracles, and the efficacy of the sacred; yet, for some unexplained reason, the citizen still believes and likes to believe in a power above the manifest power. Those who theorize about politics, Burdeau seems to hold, must therefore assume—following a course somewhere between rationality and irrationality— that this metapower is embodied in the state, although we cannot say exactly why this is so. Yet this ignorance authorizes us to turn our back on the concept of sacralized power.

11. Burdeau, *L'Etat* (Paris: Éditions du Seuil, 1970), 77.

We have here an almost magical operation by an important proponent of the modern desacralized state. In fact, we have another myth by which the state may be harnessed by the technological ideology. Burdeau's point is that Western democracies trust that the complexity of modern life, above all the complexity of the economy, creates societal relationships as substitutes for lost spiritual homogeneity. "Things happen," he writes, "as if technological society had achieved such a domination over the public mentality that the state itself is seen merely as a functioning mechanism"—in other words, as devoid of sacrality and power.[12]

Burdeau is not alone as a representative of the modern political vacillation between power with a residual sacrality and technological power. On the one hand, he and others regard it as axiomatic that citizens are intellectually emancipated people — otherwise why educate and inform them for the performance of their democratic tasks? On the other hand, the same individualism and rationality we expect the citizens to assert also fills the community with conflict and dismantles the state. If, then, the state continues to exist, there must be a component in its makeup that is not purely rational, that still consists of mystery and sacrality. Although it may cost a great deal to acknowledge it, we must postulate the survival of a remnant of the "mythological" that evolution has not yet abolished. Burdeau summarizes the process briefly: "As the governing charisma slowly fell apart, another, rationally based, belief took over. . . . Although mythology has been eliminated, the state has remained the place of a new myth."[13]

Henceforth, the question is what to do with the residual sacred? Should we acknowledge it as an obstinate core of the political construct that resists destruction by evolutionary forces, or should we minimize its importance and pare it down in size? Neither way

12. Ibid., 145.
13. Ibid., 78. It is interesting to remember that Spinoza's attacks on positive religion, in his case Judaism, contained the same arguments. Miracles, mysteries, and divine inspiration were to be eliminated as superstition, and a sober, rational religion, with mostly ethical contents, was to be established. Spinoza's influence on Lessing, Kant, Hegel, and Goethe was, in this respect, extremely important. In Burdeau's thesis the attempt to demythify the state is the same as Spinoza's attempt to desacralize religion. For Spinoza's views on the matter, see chiefly his *Tractatus theologico-politicus.*

would come to terms with power or with the sacred. Burdeau holds that "power is a curse" and that rational people have but one option toward it: to "emancipate themselves at least from the humiliations that power inflicts, by taming the mystery of authority."[14] Perhaps the authority of the state can be tamed—the history of contemporary civil society may even be labeled "the taming of the state." But political power as such will not go away for all that; it will only withdraw to its feudalistic forms and abstain from advertising itself as power (see Chapter Five). Yet no reconstruction of political power is conceivable without the sacred embedded in it. What the formulators of a new sacred and of the future of power have in mind is rather a kind of collective therapy, an ideal generated by the evolutionary hope of a society without power and without the sacred. This is how Georges Balandier imagines the shape of the new society: "Modernity arrives with a new equipment, calling forth qualitative and quantitative changes in the collective representation. A new consciousness arises, the grasp of a different historical process; the upheavals lead to new relationships with other social partners."[15]

Is technological mastery sufficient for society's stabilization and for the concomitant elimination of the sacred? What this notion ignores, among other things, is that the arrival of a "new equipment" prompts at once a new struggle over its ownership and use. After all, "new equipment" translates differently into capitalist and Marxist language. In the latter it is read as the "means of production," and it is the chief spoil in the war of classes. In capitalist language it means the formation of competing business feudalities.[16]

14. Burdeau, *L'Etat*, 79.

15. Balandier, *Le détour, pouvoir et modernité* (Paris: Éditions Fayard, 1985), 143.

16. It is noteworthy that many credit technology with bringing the new salvation—and first of all consensus, peace, and universal cooperation. They forget that new technologies and "new equipments" always brought competition and war, the will to possess a monopoly. The new techniques of safer navigation in the fifteenth century, for example, brought rivalry between Spain and Portugal, and later England, France, and the Netherlands. Modern industry led to Anglo-German competition, later to war. A current example is the Soviet-American rivalry for the military and industrial domination of space.

The study of ancient societies has taught contemporary anthropologists and political scientists that the participation of symbols and rituals is vital for society's self-understanding and equilibrium. In proportion as the state is bereft of these sacred components, which explain and limit its power, it becomes mechanical and impersonal, a cold monster. When the state depended on animated and familiar forces, the sacrifices it demanded may have been often cruel and violent, but they were at least understood by the citizens who knew themselves to be integrated into the same cosmos as the ruler. Today, when the citizens are told that *they* are the rulers and carriers of supreme responsibility, it is difficult for them to reconcile suffering and victimization, ineluctable evils in all communities of human beings, with the concept of a rational and scientific government.[17]

It is not hard to reach a diagnosis: we cannot produce a new sacred, and we cannot revive the traditional one. To be sure, there are some constants in our present estimation of the sacred and its links with our aspirations and needs. Few people now deny, after two centuries of gradual desacralization, that "power requires a representation, a decorum, pomp and ceremony, and a distance between ruler and subject," but even Balandier whom I quote would not go so far as to make the necessary parallel point: it is impossible to expect the presence of these constants in the community without a fully valued sacred. The most he concedes is the optimistic view of some "new sacred," this time in an autonomous society, which would guarantee smooth functioning, without upheavals and violent changes of orientation. Such a controlled immanence—no one ever says what controlls it—could not be established under a sacred presence; it is a modern ideal, closest per-

---

17. Partly to answer this contradiction within the modern liberal-democratic state and partly to restore a substitute for the sacred, some thinkers in the nineteenth and twentieth centuries attempted to rehabilitate the *nation*—with unifying characteristics far surpassing the merely political—as an entity capable of satisfying peoples' deep aspirations. The nation-state lent itself to this role: it was a framework of symbols, it reached to the past for roots, and, whether imperial Japan, czarist Russia, or monarchic France, it was perceived as a divinely founded and protected community, a quasi-homogeneous milieu.

haps to Alexis de Tocqueville's Tutelary State. What Balandier
and others mistake here for the sacred is a self-generated predic-
tion of uniform and indefinite progress on the plane of technology.
These political therapists commit an error of calculation, however,
when they assume that "moral progress" will spring up from some
unidentified source to accompany technological progress. This
deus ex machina, this leap into utopia, is the last desperate formulation intended to forestall the necessity—although it remains an
impossibility—of restoring the sacred.

*   *   *

The sacred world consisted of two layers of vastly unequal substance and value: the world of the real (of the gods, of cosmic es-
sences and forces, of the eternal model) and its mundane replica at
a lower degree of reality. Between the two, there circulated influences, emanations, and mediations, represented as angels, magical
beings, spirits, devils, and myriad others. Communication between
the two levels was alive and active, mainly because the two were
parts of one cosmos, and each was attentive and attuned to the other,
without doubt being cast on the superiority of one over the other.
This ontological difference, still compatible with an operational
harmony, permitted the presence in both cult and culture of myth,
through which the lower world came to terms with the higher.

Eric Voegelin explains how the God of Isaiah and Paul, and the
God of Plato, broke through the cosmological myths in which the
gods represented human experience.[18] This breakthrough is a break
with nature and cosmos, which became henceforth desacralized
and empty; it is at the same time the changeover to the incarnate
Christ, thereafter the only sacred and the only object of imitation.
The history of the West after this central event has been a variously
interpreted follow-up on the initial act of desacralization: the new
civilization felt justified in choosing its own response to the call to
imitate Christ. Jaroslav Pelikan, in his intriguing work *Jesus
through the Centuries,* lists no fewer than eighteen different cultural, political, and artistic aspects of the Jesus figure. In the course
of two thousand years, Christians have had ample opportunities to

18. I refer to Voegelin's manuscript "The Gospel and Culture."

imitate Christ *in their own way,* and the process still continues. Many of these imitations are patently untrue to the original; they may be materialistic or violent or falsely spiritual. But this was the risk that Christianity had to take, and took. The moral relationship with Christ, the relationship of faith, is by its nature free. Humanity is challenged in depth and is thereby free and mobile to change history according to opportunity and insight. This relationship was not accompanied by any guarantee that God would remain in focus, or that humanity would not break through the limits he had set. In fact, we may read Western history as the periodic redefinition of these limits.[19] The redefined limits are then often sacralized. We have clearly moved quite a distance from communities with a fixed sacred, which was interpreted through immutable rituals according to the dictation of a never-changing model.

Many thinkers today accuse Christianity of having thoughtlessly dismantled the pre-Christian cosmos in which people used to live in a satisfying comprehension of the gods, of nature, of history, and of themselves. Christ's religion opened the gates, and pandemonium ensued. There rushed in not the spirits and the daemons of the ancient world, however, but the demiurges of a mechanical universe, the negators of morality and the soul, the demythifiers, the grim-jawed iconoclasts, the corroders of mystery and power. It is natural to ask whether this situation in humanity's spiritual vision and in the community's order may be reversed, since the two are interdependent. In other words: Must the political order be derived from a cosmic model (or, at any rate, from a external, transcendent reference point), or are there valid and effective substitutes? Can unaided humanity, through the mobilization of its faculties, create a sacred, or at least a myth, powerful enough to convey a model? If the answer to these questions is no, we must then ask: Can a community exist without the sacred component, by the mere power of rational decisions and intellectual discourse?

19. Liberation theology is one of the latest redefinitions of the limits of God and the moral law. The theologians of South America and their European mentors argue that Christ came for the poor (as Marx defines the term), that he was violently antirich and against power ("anti-imperialist," as Moscow defines the term), and that any means, including revolution, may meet God's approval provided they change the social structures.

In earlier chapters we did in fact answer the first two questions with no. There are no substitutes for the sacred, even as there is no substitute for transcendence. Nor is humanity able to invent, propose, or formulate a new sacred; the sacred comes (or does not come) to us from transcendent reality. In response to the third question—whether a community can be entirely devoid of the sacred and be entirely rational—all we can say is that we do not know, since we have never before tried. We have seen that important thinkers are attempting to circumvent this immense problem by proposing that the authority of the citizens' freedom and judgment alone is sufficient for a no-longer sacralized state to order political existence—that is, that no higher authority is necessary.[20]

This is, however, like lifting oneself up by one's own bootstraps. The result can be only short-lived arrangements—arrangements that in the citizens' mind have only an unfounded existence—while the state evacuates its residual sacred and mobilizes the dynamics of individualism. The benefits of such an arrangement are derived from contracts and from the mechanization and automation of all relationships.[21] The ultimate logic of liberal industrial society leads

20. On the other hand, there is at the same time a vast and serious literature in which such brilliant writers as Aldous Huxley, George Orwell, Evgeny Zamiatin, and Alexander Zinoviev suggest that society's desacralization leads to the mechanical efficiency and robotization of humanity. Such literature, which takes aim at the utopia of the demythifiers, never existed before—it is a true invention of our century. While Huxley and Orwell send out alarm signals, the more recent conclusion of Zinoviev is somewhat different. He sees that in the modern view human beings have—and need—no responsibility, no initiative, no concern except for undisturbed material survival. Not only is this the Soviet ideal, but he sees evidence that the symptoms have spread to the West as well. We may legitimately ask: If we feel pity for the man of sacral civilizations, what should our sentiments be vis-à-vis the desacralized man?

21. Family relations are mechanized as mothers are free to refuse the shelter of their womb to the fetus; homosexuals are free to marry and adopt children; former lovers are required to pay alimony. The mechanization of physician-patient relations is apparent in the increasing litigation under malpractice laws and the growth of walk-in medical-care centers. Doctors here are piece workers, obliged to work fast so as to make profit for the employer. Teacher-student relations are mechanized by the continual student evaluations of their professors' competence and attitude and the reasonableness of

us back to the Hobbesian nightmare, *bellum omnium contra omnes* (the war of everyone against everyone). What for the British philosopher was a useful myth, never actually experienced by humanity, has become a concrete reality in our desacralized milieu.

---

their requirements. The consequence of all this is a quasi-Orwellian fear and conformism, depersonalization, hidden bitterness, distrust, resentment, hostility, and conflict.

Some Philosophical Considerations

One may have formed the impression that not only have I described here the confrontation between two very different sorts of human culture and two concepts of power but I have also expressed a preference for one over the other. I would like now to comment on that impression. We often hear or read today of discussions that claim to be free of what is called a "value judgment." Yet such discussions or descriptions usually do express, contrary to their claim, a value. A medical report about a man's illness is one thing; the description of an involved witness, say a family member, of that man's suffering is something completely different. Just as that witness—nay, participant—inserts a value judgment into the description of the illness, we all, as participants in the course of Western culture, insert value judgments into our reflection on the questions I have raised here.

If the participants in the debate of our century have contested any one subject more heatedly than the famous ideological battles between Marxism, capitalism, fascism, and liberalism, it is likely this question of questions: Will Western civilization survive? Indeed, there is not a single influential thinker in the last one hundred fifty years who did not devote the essential part of his thought to this one problem—note just the work of Jakob Burckhardt, Friedrich Nietzsche, Edmund Husserl, Paul Valéry, Oswald

Spengler, Arnold Toynbee, Martin Heidegger, Christopher Dawson, and an as-yet endless succession of others.

We may distinguish two broad schools in this ever-swelling legion. The first includes those who are generally satisfed with the course of Western civilization and see in its modern forms a healthy correction of older, traditional, and obscure if not obscurantist ways and attitudes. They are optimistic because they believe that what they see as a linear course of civilization will continue into an ever more satisfying and enlightened future. Facing them is the school of those who see a tragic rupture at several past junctures, who diagnose the present as having lost the substance in which all past civilizations shared, and who see humanity's future, at least in the short run, as robotized, the divine spark dimmed.

Two types of people are absent from this controversy, which often intensifies into a battle: the happy hedonists, indifferent to all except their personal, mostly material, contentment here and now and the strong believers who stand above the vicissitudes of contemporary civilization and history, convinced that all that matters is the final triumph of the faith, of which they are unshakeably convinced.

The viewpoint I have taken in this book is that civilization matters because its forms depend on something more than human decisions: civilization depends on humanity's connection with transcendent reality. This connection is expressed by the ultimately sacral character of civilization, a living force which permeates, in various degrees, human institutions, moral attitudes, artistic visions, and manifestations of political power.[1] These expressions are not at all abstract; they are observable, almost tangible public objects, and they exert in turn an influence on public and private

---

1. This solidarity of forms in a sacral civilization is luminously expressed in a book on Russian icons: "The architectural character of the icon expresses one of its central, essential ideas, the idea of universal communality. The dominance of architectural lines over the human form expresses man's subordination to the communal, the preponderance of the universal over the individual. Man here ceases to be a self-contained person and submits to the overall design." Eugene N. Trubetskoi, *Icons: Theology in Color* (Crestwood, N.Y.: St. Vladimir's Seminary Press, 1973), 26-27.

life. Only the saint and the sinner may situate themselves *outside* these expressions of a civilization—but they seldom do. They know that civilization demands participation at every level, from participation in the sacred to participation in judgment of the course of civilization itself.

This is to say that one cannot pass value-free judgments on values. Nobody ever did, not even when using clichés and slogans claiming to do so. Those who claim to speak objectively merely put a positive sign on the civilization in which they live: they do not see values for what they are but call them facts, signifying thereby their uncritical satisfaction.

Having said this much in justification of the thesis of this book—that power and all of Western civilization has been and continues to be desacralized—we are called to go one step farther. If, as I believe, the attempts to sacralize science, technology, and popular sovereignty have proved successive failures, how do we escape our predicament? It is one thing to post a "no exit" sign and declare that our civilization and ours alone has been launched on a rough, one-way road and that we have now reached its end. It is another thing to set about locating a new sacred, that is, a new civilization—a new road out. Such an enterprise, however, is rendered impossible under the thesis I have adopted here. The sacred cannot be solicited, and therefore civilizations, with their sacred nucleus, cannot be approximated, planned, or outlined in advance, let alone prescribed. This would be feasible only if the cyclical view of history were correct and past configurations regularly returned. But this pre-Christian view is a view we no longer accept; Greek, Judaic, and Christian civilizations have broken with the circular, thus static, vision and entered long ago on the linear course with its dynamism, now turning *in vacuo*.

Addressing himself to the European side of this problematic, the Czech philosopher Jan Patocka speaks of the Platonic "care of the soul" that modernity has lost.[2] Care of the soul is that movement of the inner life which carries us beyond the observed phe-

---

2. Patocka, *Platon et l'Europe* (Paris: Éditions Verdier, 1983). This work contains the text of a semiclandestine seminary course held in Prague in 1973.

nomena to their essence—to their sacrality, we might say. If the soul, God's eminent creation, possesses such a dynamism of its own—and Plato intended his entire oeuvre as an illustration of this—then it may at any time, again and again, humbly request divine assistance. The soul, at all times a rectifier of matter, appears as the only conceivable counterpoint to the material dynamics implicit in the linear course of history. The sentence contains no program of civilization; it contains something better: hope.

Index of Names